8.95

THE CONNOISSEUR'S BOOK

OF THE CIGAR

THE CONNOISSEUR'S BOOK OF

THE Cigar.

BY

Z. Davidoff

WITH THE
COLLABORATION OF
GILLES LAMBERT

TRANSLATED
FROM THE FRENCH BY
LAWRENCE GROW

McGraw-Hill

BOOK COMPANY

NEW YORK
ST. LOUIS
SAN FRANCISCO
TORONTO
MEXICO CITY
PANAMA

Art Direction: Harris Lewine
Design: Seymour Chwast

Library of Congress Catalog Card Number: 73-92696

FIRST EDITION
45678   VBVB   9876
15460

INTRODUCTION

GLORIAS DE   GUILLERMO II.

The experienced, mature man who is able to advise the young is a fortunate and happy individual. When I was twenty, I fell in love with the great tobacco plantations in Cuba. This passion of my youth has never been spent. Today, I am able to say that my life has been placed under the sign of service to all those who are dedicated to the cigar—young or old. The cigar has been my life. I owe it everything: my pleasures and my anguish, the joys of my work as well as the pleasant leisure hours it affords, and, if I have acquired over the course of the years some bit of philosophical perspective, it is again to the cigar that I am in debt.

Such talk may seem amusing. It should. The cigar is an instrument of happiness and carries with it, as time passes, relaxation and peace of mind. In the beginning, I smoked like a glutton. My parents were cigar merchants in Kiev. My father's store was a small one and all the family made cigarettes by hand, cigarettes with gold tips and filled with blond tobacco imported from Turkey. This store was not like any other. From time to time, bizarre gentlemen with conspiratorial looks would gather there. They *were* conspirators. And just as the liberator of Cuba, José Martí, exiled in Florida, used to send messages rolled in cigars, so the enemies of the Czars in Kiev carried out their plans behind a cigar-smoke screen. Eventually the conspiratorial ring was discovered and I, with my family, left Russia in a covered wagon. In Geneva my father opened a small workshop and began again to build up a trade. Other exiles came to the shop. They were feverishly preparing for the revolution. One of them greatly impressed me. He had a thin face, brilliant eyes, and spoke in a loud voice. He also took cigars and didn't pay for them. My father never tried to recover the money. On a bill which I have kept as a souvenir are stamped the words *Not Paid* and the name of this customer—Vladimir Ulyanov. Not until later was he known as Lenin.

I did not leave my father's shop until he encouraged me to take a trip to the Americas in order to learn something about the tobacco trade. "I am not able to give you much money," he said, "only some letters of introduction to tobacco merchants. But if you use them correctly, these letters are worth gold. In our business, friendship is not a vain word." I learned very quickly what he meant by friendship, this solidarity which unites men of tobacco—growers, merchants, and devotees—in all countries. I spent some time in Buenos Aires and was warmly welcomed there. In Brazil I discovered black tobacco—the tobacco of cigars. In the East leaves are too small and fragile to be used in making cigars. This had been a revelation to me; I understood for the first time that the greatness of our craft was to be found in the large, strong, luxuriant leaves.

For several months I worked on the rich and ravishing plantations in the state of Bahia. One day an old Brazilian planter I respected told me: "Son, you love tobacco. Go to Cuba—to the land of the red clay soil. There you will discover the *puro*, the pure cigar. Then, nothing else will exist for you."

I left for Cuba in the state of anticipation a young archeologist might for Greece or a seminarian for Rome. For two years I stayed there, wrapped in a veritable state of excitement which affected all the senses. I worked on a *finca* and was initiated into all the aspects of manufacturing the *puro,* the cigar—from the cutting of the plant to the packaging, through the stages of gathering the leaf, fermentation, drying, dividing, and rolling. I was curious about everything and not satisfied until I knew everything there was to know about a Havana. I talked to old laborers who had been witnesses, in their youth, to the first efforts of European colonizers to develop a market for cigars. I learned very quickly that just as there are no two great wines which are the same, no two cigars are identical. I soon learned, thanks to the workers, to distinguish between a cigar made with the leaves from the top of the plant and one made from leaves to be found lower down, between cigars from different areas and of different years. Eventually I knew which were the best cigars in the world—and why.

4

INTRODUCTION

When I returned to Europe I decided to dedicate my talents to the tobacco business. The *puro* of Cuba is not a cigar like any other. Even when boxed, it continues to mature, to "live." It has several requirements. It is the king of the tobacco products and should be treated according to its rank. In Switzerland, soon after my return I installed several humidified storage rooms (caves). I made the first of the humidors. And to the concern of my family—from whom tobacco had never required such treatment—I started out on an adventure I have never regretted.

Some of the most famous men in the world have come to my store and, as well, less illustrious lovers of the cigar who know to ask the right question: "Monsieur Davidoff, what are your best cigars?" I have given kings, princes, and millionaires the great pleasure of choosing the right cigar. Great ladies have come into the back rooms to sample the latest shipments. I have had to refuse service to valets because no honest man will have his servant choose his cigars. When I open my order books I realize that there is not a man on earth who has among his clientele—and his friends—more kings, dukes, millionaires, adventurers, celebrities—or beautiful women. We are brought together by a common bond—the cigar. In Cuba it is said that no hatred exists on the land of the tobacco plantations. I see the land of black tobacco in my dreaming moments, a land viewed through clouds of blue smoke: Bahía, Alquízar, Candelaria, San Luis Padrón, Orojo, Atoquia, Pinar del Río, the western province of Cuba containing the celebrated Vuelta Abajo—the sacred square of ochre-red. My natural home; my home of adoption. I came from the East, from the cold, the plains battered by winds from the steppes. I discovered Cuba's perfume and her sensual warmth as an immature adolescent discovers an ardent, knowledgeable woman.

Today, at home when I light a cigar taken from my own personal stock, I feel a marvelous sense of contentment. The same feeling, I imagine, is felt by those who have not sought

5

to understand the mysteries of black tobacco but who enjoy a good cigar in the evening, after a pleasant dinner with good friends. Sublime moments. Precious moments, and like the smoke that rises from the gray ash, fleeting but unforgettable ones.

Stendhal—who smoked Italian cigars (Toscani)—wrote that those who have known the feeling of happiness four or five times in their lives should feel gratified. A good cigar brings one closer to such a state. There is, in the pleasure a good cigar gives, something indefinable that has never ceased to puzzle me. I have thought of it a great deal. I think I have considered everything —the promise of barely mature leaf to that of a complicated mixture. Yet it is a matter I will continue to ponder and, without a doubt, ponder for a long time. What is there in a cigar that intensifies and prolongs the pleasure of smoking, which so attracts men? What is the noble quality the cigar brings to tobacco—to the light intoxication of a dried plant? How can one say that the cigar—nothing but an object—has a soul?

I have sought answers in history books. Commerce in tobacco began longer ago than the memory of living men. It seems that the plant made its appearance long ago in Yucatán. At the time of its discovery by Westerners in the sixteenth century, it may already have been smoked for over ten centuries. How? No one knows. But it was the cigar that Columbus' sailors discovered. The Indians do not move about (it is written in Columbus' journal) without *un tizón en la mano y yerbas para tomar sus sahumerios que acostumbran* (a torch in the hand and herbs from which they taste the smoke).

It was in the form of a cigar that use of the Indian plant spread in Spain and Portugal. Curiously, use of the cigar did not extend beyond the borders of these two kingdoms, leaving only snuff-taking and pipe-smoking for the less favored. Two centuries later the torch of the Indians, perfected and enlarged, became the *puro,* the pure cigar of the Spanish, and it was adopted by people beyond the Pyrenees.

INTRODUCTION

The Indian cigar was not for everyone! Experts claim that in Yucatán it was reserved for the pleasure of the king and priests. Its magic smoke constituted, it is said, a privileged access to invisible powers. This is also the thought of a contemporary philosopher, Claude Levi-Straus. In a recent book, *Du Miel aux cendres,* he explains that tobacco has always been an instrument of communication with the supernatural.

What is certain is that in Europe—especially in Spain and Portugal—the cigar was a privilege enjoyed by the nobility. It was smoked in the Court, in the princely palaces where the gold of the Conquest was displayed. The cigar was more than a pleasurable object; it was a symbol of wealth. Only slowly did it lose this significance. Later, it was a symbol of success, especially that enjoyed by the *nouveau riche,* the illustrious, politicians. Franz Liszt, the musical genius, never left on a trip without his personal reserve of cigars: several cases of precious wood contained the treasure. At the beginning of this century, the world powers sent ambassadors to Cuba to select the very best tobacco leaves and to survey the stock of fine cigars. Anywhere from five to ten thousand cigars were kept in storage.

As for Cuba itself, all great smokers discovered long ago the irreplaceable virtues of this magic island: its geology, wind, water, its miraculous soil. As Bernard Wolfe, the writer and cigar smoker, has written, "The Vuelta Abajo is a natural hothouse, just as the whole island of Cuba is a natural humidor." For Cubans, and for me, the *puro* can be nothing other than Cuban, nothing other than a Havana.

Much has changed in recent years, but the best cigars are the same—even if their names have been changed. Neither war nor politics has altered the cigar. Great cigars still come from the same precious land. Surviving every vicissitude, a good Havana with a gold or purple band, in its wooden box with cedar shavings, encased in its baroque splendor, is still the master of the cigar world. It cannot be cut off from its glorious past or its obscure origins. Of noble lineage, it will never be a simple manufactured object. The cigar should never be treated like a cigarette. It is something that commands respect. It is made for all the senses, for all the pleasures, for the nose, the palate, the fingers, the eyes. When rolled between the fingers, the slight cracking sound is an extra pleasure for the ears. A good cigar contains the promise of a totally pleasurable experience. "A woman is only a woman, but a good cigar is a Smoke," wrote Kipling in "The Betrothed." And George Sand: "The cigar numbs sorrow and fills the solitary hours with a million gracious images." To know how to smoke is to recover certain forgotten rhythms, to re-establish communication with the self. If there is a secret of the cigar, it is to be found in the slow movements, the dignified, measured smoking. The movements are more than mannerisms; they are ceremonial acts. "The ash of a cigar has always been sacred," wrote Eugene Marsan. "It is wrong to demand a light from those who lovingly contemplate the long ash of a Havana. . . . The conversation of cigar smoking ought to be slow and majestic. . . ."

The cigar has inspired writers and poets. I have no intention of adding to their odes. Simply, I will say that the number of artists who have recognized the romance of the cigar is many. The mysteries are difficult to explain. If tobacco is a lost cult, if the cigar is surrounded by a mystery that eludes us, it is necessary to bow before the mystery. We never know exactly why we smoke. It is imperative, however, to know *how* to smoke. "The cigar smoker," wrote critic Marc Alyn, "like the perfect lover or the bagpipe player, is a calm man, slow and sure of his wind." He is a man who knows happiness. Yet he ought to know a bit of etiquette and science in order to augment his pleasure. "Any cigar smoker is a friend," wrote Alfred de Musset in a letter, "because I know what he feels." So in formulating my ideas on how to smoke—the fruit of my experience—I am embarking on a labor of love and friendship.

8

PART ONE

The
Know-How
of the
Smoker

When you examine a well-chosen cigar, hold it between the index finger and the thumb. The subtle pleasure it offers may be anticipated by inspecting the color of the wrapper, the shape of the cigar, its length, by feeling its solidness, and by smelling its aroma. Roll it between your fingers without too much pressure. Once satisfied by its elasticity, its suppleness, examine its extremities— its head and foot—and the cigar band. These are the steps taken by a man who knows that taking the measure of a cigar before cutting or lighting it ought to be a serious matter. They are ceremonial gestures that should not be neglected.

CUTTING

Before lighting your cigar—the decisive act—you ought to cut the firm end known as the head. There are three ways of cutting a cigar: by pinching with the fingers, using the teeth, or with the aid of an instrument. No one of these methods is better than another.

Unique Rule: The opening should be small, reasonable, in proportion to the cigar, and made so that an appropriate amount of smoke will be produced. The opening ought to be clean.

Any method of cutting that respects these imperatives is admissible. American smokers, in general, use a cutter. Others—not the most sophisticated—chew off the end. Outside the fact that a very sharp cut is required (and this may call for two or three bites), this method does not permit much precision. I realize that some smokers are past masters of this technique, but I never practice or recommend such a method. One takes few risks when pinching the end. If the fingernail is long and sharp enough, a simple slit (one-sixth of an inch for a Corona) can be made in the wrapper. This detail is important. The cut made with the nail should not be too wide or too deep. This should not be difficult since a Havana in good condition is easy to pierce. If the cigar is a little dry, I suggest wetting the end of it in the

11

mouth. Years ago, when the fashionable cigar was a dry, crackly Dutch one (Havanas were reserved for the illustrious), it was simple, after having wet the end, to crumple the cigar between the thumb and index finger in the same way as rolling. A piece of the wrapper became detached from the end and, after having cut the under wrapper, the opening was sufficient to obtain a good draw. This method can also be used for a dry cigar, but in this case it is preferable to cut normally after having moistened the head.

This advice is also useful if you use a cigar cutter. Despite the opinion of some, it is not shameful to use such an instrument, especially if it has been well chosen. Ordinary cigar cutters, which make a round or beveled cut, are not to be condemned. Sometimes, however, you must watch that the cut is not made too deeply. Do not forget that the beveled cut produces more drawing surface than the superficial circle opening.

Cigar cutters are fine, but *not* the penknife or the lance, which savagely pierce the delicate head of the cigar, thereby creating a useless funnel for an excess of heat, tar-filled smoke, and a bitter taste.

LIGHTING

The moment has come to bring the cigar to the lips and to proceed to the delicate operation of lighting it. This is also the time to dismiss certain errors, false theories, and dangerous legends. Just recently I read a series of complicated pointers for cigar smoking that completely confounded me. These were printed in a mass-circulation magazine. To begin with, the "expert" recommended that the cigar be warmed all along its flank with a match, lighter, or candle (!) before lighting. After this, he advised lighting the foot of the cigar. Alas, this pratice is still followed in many elegant restaurants. It is an anachronism. Until the end of the nineteenth century, the wrappers of certain Spanish cigars were stained with a special gum the color of chicory.

THE KNOW-HOW OF THE SMOKER

Then it was wise to eliminate the taste of the gum by heating the cigar before lighting. Today, the vegetable gum used to seal the wrapper to the ends is without odor, and I see no advantage in continuing the practice. Rather, it only presents risks and inconvenience. In any case, one never warms more than the exterior of a cigar, and this should not modify the temperature of the smoke. I recommend only that you warm the foot very lightly—several seconds—before bringing it to your lips. This creates an entryway for the smoke. The first puff you draw will then be free of some residual odors.

What kind of flame should be used in lighting? I say anything except that produced by a gasoline lighter or a sulphur or wax match. Use a wooden match, a gas lighter, or a wood shaving. The important thing is that the source of light should be used with care.

A strong habit indulged by some smokers—not amateurs—is to use strips from the layer of cedar in boxes of good cigars. Actually, the means of lighting has no influence from the point of view of the quality or quantity of the first puffs you draw from a cigar. The cedar shavings, however, should be used with care because of the hot flame they produce. The flame, in effect, ought to be small. You do not light a cigar with a fire. The flame should never actually touch the cigar. With the cigar in your mouth, rotate the flame around the tuck (the opened end) until first there is a red rim and then an evenly burning coal. Very quickly, a small fire is lit and it grows in intensity, spreading its smoke through the filler. Except for some accident, the fire should be well established. Such is the respect that I hold for the British royal family —who have been and continue to be with Prince Philip and Lord Snowdon true devotees of the cigar—that I refuse to give them the advice Edward VII profferred to a young lord in his entourage: pierce the cigar with a lance and, after lighting it, wave it in the air.

If you use a match, keep a second handy because it is most likely

13

that it will take two lights to get the necessary fire. Sometimes it may even be necessary to use three matches, especially if the cigar is fresh. Do not ask another man for a light. The lighting of a cigar should be a personal affair. To ask for assistance is to create a relation of dependence. The conqueror Bismarck, one day in 1870, was riding without an escort in Paris' Bois de Boulogne. He sensed no feeling of animosity around him. Suddenly, he heard some angry shouting. The situation could have turned out badly. Bismarck pulled out a cigar, pulled on the reins, and demanded a light from a passerby. The fellow hesitated, but the imperious look of the Chancellor was too much. How could the fellow refuse Bismarck a light, even if he was a hated enemy? The man produced his tinder lighter and lit the cigar. The cries died down. Bismarck and his cigar had won the country. The promenade of the conqueror continued in silence and a cloud of smoke.

Rules: A cigar ought not to be lighted too quickly or too slowly but evenly, in small puffs. A successful light lays the ground for a regular and even smoke.

When lighting, the cigar should be kept around a third of an inch from the flame.

If the cigar has been well lighted, the first long puff will be better than those to follow. Lighting is a serious and discrete act. It is an act that requires care and excludes exhibitionism.

RELIGHTING

Contrary to the opinion of some, it is not shameful to let a cigar go out. It is only clumsy and awkward. You can (and ought to) relight the cigar as soon as it has gone out. This you should do if less than half of the cigar has been smoked. Decide for yourself if less than half but more than a quarter has been smoked. If less than a quarter of the cigar is left, give it up. A smoker of taste will never attempt to relight a cigar of such short length.

THE KNOW-HOW OF THE SMOKER

To relight a cigar, do not put it in your mouth. Using a match or other object, scratch the burned end. Then hold the cigar between your fingers and present it to the flame, turning it for two or three seconds. This slight reheating is necessary and should be sufficient. The cigar "repairs" itself without puffing. Now, after this relighting, all should be the same as before. There will be no disagreeable smell or inconvenience. The same aroma will reappear, and the same delicious pleasure.

You can relight a cigar two or three times. But in any case, do consider the possibility that there has been some fault in the manufacturing. It may not be your fault.

THE BAND

Should you remove the band before lighting the cigar or right away after lighting, or should you smoke the cigar with the band? On this point there are many different thoughts. "What voluptuousness," wrote Mallarmé, "when I lunched with my father, in the last century, at *Bignon* or *Paillard*. After finishing the meal, he produced boxes of sparkling cigars: Valle, Clay, Upmann. I opened these boxes which evoked visions of dancing girls, and I removed the bands, *because that is what is to be done....*" and Paul Bouguet: "The count, a sophisticated man, crushed his half-smoked Havana in the ashtray, and then took care to destroy the band which had *remained* on it." Decide for yourself what is right!

A little bit of history will shed some light on the subject. It is said that the cigar band was invented by Gustave Bock, one of the first Europeans to settle in Cuba and the man who helped build the Cuban cigar industry. The band had a triple function: to hold together the wrapper in case there was not enough gum on it to bind the ends, to protect delicate fingers from a very problematic deposit of nicotine, and, finally, to mark the (always excellent) products of Mr. Bock. Until the invention of the band at the end of the last century, cigars were sometimes tied together in bunches with a silk ribbon. The little emblem of colored paper was to do much to increase the popularity of the cigar.

Today, the risk of the wrapper coming undone has almost disappeared, and with it the danger of soiling the fingers with nicotine or any other product of burning tobacco. But the ingenious idea of Mr. Bock survives. The band is now in general use; it has acquired an artistic dimension—baroque and lyrical. It has attained the level of a precious object. I have seen some sumptuous bands designed by great painters. I have also seen them decorated with gold, ostrich plumes, diamond fragments. Fantastic prices have been received for some collections containing thousands of examples.

Sensitive as I am to this poetry of the band, I do recommend removing it after lighting the cigar, that is, after having smoked about a fifth of the cigar. By that time the cigar will have attained its "cruising speed." There is little or no chance that the wrapper will slowly come undone. In any case, the cigar is even more attractive in its nudity. The purity of its line will be more clearly seen. Do remove the band delicately. If it is in any way attached to the wrapper, raise and remove the band with your fingernail, taking care not to rip the fragile wrapper.

If you prefer to smoke a cigar with its band to the halfway point or even three-quarters, go right ahead. It is not an offensive practice, and don't be upset by those who reproach you; there is nothing of bad taste or vulgarity in this habit. So far as I know, there is not any sort of fetishism either. I would only add that there are some excellent cigars without bands—often the best cigars—and some frightful ones decorated with gold or purple bands.

HOW TO HOLD A CIGAR IN THE MOUTH

The cigar is held firmly in the mouth, but not strongly. One should not clench a cigar between the teeth, and certainly not hold it at a slant. Certain smokers have the curious habit of sticking a toothpick or matchstick in the end of the cigar to help hold it in the mouth. They also say that it improves the draw. I am not able even to talk about this aberration.

Try to keep the end in your mouth as dry as possible. Avoid chewing on it or drawing in your tongue. Saliva on the end of a cigar is a disgusting sight, and is hardly less nauseating than the quid of spit and tobacco some men spit out. The sight of a wet, viscous crushed cigar is depressing for the smoker—and for those around him.

Use a cigar holder? No, please don't. Who would want to drink a good wine with a straw?

DO NOT SMOKE TOO QUICKLY

First rule: A cigar should be smoked slowly. Each person, to be sure, ought to discover his own rhythm or pace, for his greatest pleasure. It seems interesting to me, however, to provide some guidelines to go by.

The average cigar, such as the Corona, is around five inches long. Smoked normally—at least half—it ought to last at least fifty to sixty minutes. It should produce around fifty puffs, that is to say about one a minute.

Auguste Barthélemy, the author of an extraordinary book (*L'Art de fumer pipe et cigare*) written in Alexandrine verse and published in Paris in 1849, recognized the need for slowness:

> It is necessary to know how to smoke so that one knows how to choose.
> The true smoker abstains from imitating Vesuvius.
> He demonstrates the requirement that during three-quarters of an hour
> A cigar rests in his hand without going out.

In our nervous, rushed, agitated world, I have observed many smokers who follow a much faster cadence. They are fools! The faster one smokes, the less the pleasure. I am forced to remind my clients and my friends: smoke easily, nobly, peacefully, with

17

grace! Pleasure diminishes proportionately with the rise in temperature, overheating. A cigar is not something to rush through. Experience proves that you must learn *how* to smoke a cigar. The unfortunate Charles Bovary whom Gustave Flaubert made famous was made the object of pity by his wife because he smoked so badly—too fast and grossly "in advancing the lips, spitting each minute, drawing back at each puff."

A CIGAR IS ALSO TO BE SMOKED WITH THE FINGERS

The cigar should not be kept in the mouth all the time, contrary to a practice that unhappily has developed. The cigar should symbolize repose, relaxation, leisure. A cigar ought not to be smoked solely with the mouth, but with the hand, the eyes, and with the spirit. Each puff carries its own pleasure. The cigar, faithful to its aristocratic bearing, should not be smoked while working. It is a luxury item. It requires attention, dignity, and taste—and a group of movements that exclude all other physical activity.

First rule: Before taking a cigar, be sure that your hands are clean and free of any odor. Pay particular attention to cologne or lighter fluid.

A cigar ought not to be held between the index and middle fingers as is a cigarette, but between the index finger and the thumb. Winston Churchill did not follow this advice, but he is pardoned. The V made with the index and middle fingers became his mark. Hold the cigar in the mouth only long enough to take a puff and for several seconds following the taste. In the time that it takes to smoke a cigar (fifty minutes), it stays in the mouth, on the average, no more than three minutes.

The rest of the time the cigar will remain immobile in your hands, parallel to the ground. Do not smoke when walking, unless it is a special cigar made for this purpose. You will not be able to talk a great deal. You sample the cigar; you are immersed in it. You do not fit a cigar into your schedule; you give it a moment and it occupies your time and enriches it.

SMOKING

The smoke of a cigar is not inhaled. The volume of smoke in the mouth produces an intense and sufficient pleasure. This peculiarity of the cigar—unlike cigarettes—keeps the smoker from all sorts of inconveniences, not to speak of risks. The membranes of the mouth, in effect, do not absorb tar and nicotine from the cigar as the membranes of the lungs do from cigarettes. It should also be said that the tobacco leaf used for cigars has much less nicotine than that found in cigarettes. The advantage of the cigar over all other tobacco products should be quite apparent. I have done a great deal of research on this problem—the reading of medical analyses and the famous Terry Report published several years ago by the U.S. Surgeon General, which was very favorable to the cigar. Several figures seem to me particularly convincing: surface of resorption for the cigarette (that is to say, with inhalation), fifty square meters of membranes. Surface of resorption for the cigar (smoke rests in the mouth), one hundred square centimeters. For me the problem is taken care of: from the point of view of absorption in the organism of nicotine and other residual substances, the cigar represents the cleanest of the tobacco "crutches."

The smoke of a well-chosen cigar should be fresh when it enters the mouth. This sense of freshness is marvelous. It is explained by the relatively low burning temperature of the cigar (in any case, much lower than that of a cigarette). Keep the smoke in your mouth for several seconds. Savor the aroma, and try to distinguish the most subtle nuances. The smoke of a good cigar has a thousand of them. There is always something new to discover. Just as no two cigars are alike, so there are no two identical aromas.

The smoke from a Havana is unique. Its aroma, flavor, color, lightness, delicacy, and its whirls of smoke are not to be equaled. From the point of view of biological science, its effects are not yet well known. Specialists who have studied this problem have not yet reached a consensus. Among the effects observed is the excitation of mood, but this matter of light intoxication is still a matter of controversy. It is normal that the smoke from the rolled leaf of tobacco—a plant related to others such as belladonna, stramonium, etc.—should exercise an effect in the psychic sphere as do aphrodisiacs. This effect was the object of a medical thesis written in Virginia in 1897 by Dr. M.E. Douglas and published in the *Homeopathic News* in the same year.

THE SMOKE OF A CIGAR IS NOT NOXIOUS

This holds true if you choose a quality cigar and do not smoke more than half of it. The first half is the best. Smoke from the remainder is increasingly strong and charged with elements. Certain smokers say that they prefer the second half for just these reasons. These individuals, to my way of thinking, are not smokers but chewers. They are the ones with bitter, damp, evil-smelling mouths. The smoke is too hot and heavily charged with the pepper of tars and resins created by the intense heat. It is this smoke doctors regard with disgust. It is no more than a caricature of itself!

THE ASH

Along with the band, the ash of the cigar shares the privilege of having given birth to an absurd fetishism and to strange taboos. How many times have I heard, in a tone of most profound gravity, "Keep from letting the ash of your cigar fall. If it does, you will commit an error, a blunder, an act of bad taste. . . ."

Error? It is wrong to think that the ash which rests at the end of the cigar acts as a thermostat on the burning core. It has no utility whatsoever. It is simply beautiful to contemplate—especially if it is found on a Havana, a gray ash which sometimes has a blue cast to it. It is a souvenir.

Bad taste? The worst thing, to my way of thinking, is to take the risk of letting the ash fall no matter when or where. Although it does not stain either fabrics or carpets, neither does it improve their condition, as another legend has it. Sacha Guitry in one of his books advises the reader to drop the ash in his palm before disposing of it in an ashtray. Guitry claims some special pleasure from this act.

I advise waiting until you see that the ash will drop off naturally by its own weight. The ash will have reached a length of an inch or so if the cigar is in good condition. The ash should fall by itself. It is vain to attempt to help nature. Do not think about it too much. The ash is of no use to you, unless you happen to be placed in the situation of a British gentleman who was accused of an indecent crime by a silly girl. He showed the policeman the long ash attached to his cigar and this proof cleared him.

Respect the ash—as you do the rest of the cigar—but do not make it an object of worship, giving it importance it does not merit. It is pretty to contemplate. It is the point of departure for the smoky spirals, the generator of dreams and oblivion. But it also represents pleasure that is past.

INCIDENTAL MATTERS

A quality cigar, well chosen and well preserved, ought to be free of any unpleasant surprises. It is possible, however, to come across an imperfection in manufacturing, as any veteran cigar smoker knows. These can be found among even those carrying the most prestigious bands. I have found cigars that are too well packed or hard (they won't stay lit despite great effort) or too soft (the smoke flows too quickly and is too hot; the cigar burns quickly). It is possible that a tired worker in a cigar factory at the end of the day has little of his usual skillfulness, his lightness of touch in a work that is as delicate as that of putting together cigars. The wrapper, or the binder leaf, both very fine, are likely to rip. The filler can contain a knot which will block the passage of the smoke. The band can adhere to the wrapper. If there is a knot, you can free it by moistening the hardest place and then by rolling it between your thumb and index finger. In principle, however, an imperfect cigar should not be smoked. Any merchant worth his name will replace it.

TO EXTINGUISH A CIGAR

A cigar smoked more than halfway extinguishes itself rapidly when you stop drawing on it. The concentration of tars dampens the fire. This natural death ought to follow after the smoking of at least half the cigar. It is a sad moment and bitter to the taste. A smoker of delicacy does not prolong it. "If the birth of a genius resembles that of an idiot," Sacha Guitry has written, "the end of a Havana Corona resembles that of a five-cent cigar."

It is, then, useless to extinguish the end of a cigar yourself—and indelicate to crush it out in an ashtray where it will leave disagreeable traces. The odor of a "cold" cigar does have a bad reputation among ladies. When out in public, get rid of the cigar remains as rapidly as possible. But let your cigar die by itself and then hide the remains.

It is wise to rest for a while after smoking a cigar. You can rinse your mouth out with coffee, tea, or a strong liqueur—cognac, framboise, kirsch, mirabelle. Some individuals appreciate particularly the resonance of a Chinese tea, which reminds them of a Havana. This is purely a question of taste. At any rate, do not light another cigar until at least ten or fifteen minutes have passed, enough time in which to savor the last cigar. "Two cigars on top of each other reveal an obsession or a brutality of the soul," wrote Eugene Marsan in his excellent book *Le Cigare*. After you have smoked a cigar, don't pick up a cigarette. After

22

even an average cigar, the best of cigarettes is bland, useless, disappointing. The pleasure of the cigar, don't forget, is not found only in the smoking. It precedes it and lingers long after the fire is out.

AND THE LADIES?

Women who smoke and know how to appreciate a good Havana are more numerous than you might think, and their number is ever on the increase. If I were not obligated to keep professional secrets, I would give some names that would surprise you. It is difficult to imagine a movie star, the symbol of female sexiness, smoking a Havana in her Mediterranean coast home, far from photographers. Geraldine Chaplin, however, was photographed at a recent Cannes film festival gracefully lighting a long Panatela. I am pleased by her choice. Such a cigar, feminine in aspect, light in flavor, seems destined for fine and perfumed fingers. We are, happily, far from the epoch of General Galliffet, a French officer of intransigent character. He had taken a position, in a most spectacular fashion, against automobiles soon after their arrival on the scene in Paris. He closed himself up in his apartment and would not venture out. In a similar manner, he forbade women to smoke cigars in his presence. At the end of a dinner, having observed a young woman lighting a small Cheroot, he walked up to her, his mustache bristling, put a protective arm around her and grumbled: "Come, my dear! *Allons pisser....*"

George Sand had some difficulty. In 1845, when she lived with Chopin on Paris' Place d'Orléans, she took her meals at the table of Madame Marliani, wife of the Spanish consul. A young Russian nobleman, W. de Lenz, who greatly admired Chopin, was not able to hide his stupefaction at seeing Madame Sand light an enormous cigar. Reportedly, their brief exchange was as follows:

"In St. Petersburg I probably would not be able to smoke a cigar in a salon."

23

"In no salon, Madame, have I ever seen a woman smoking a cigar," responded the young stranger as he backed away.

Eugene Marsan, who found the record of this conversation in Lenz's *Mémoires,* found a touching anomaly in the *Mémoires* of Las Casas, the archbishop of the Conquest. In the first version, the archbishop reported that two Spaniards, who were among the first to venture into the interior of the Indian territory and to describe the famous torches (cigars), reported that they were smoked by men and women—*mujeres y hombres.* Later, as the Indian herb became more popular, Las Casas slyly modified his text. The women disappeared from the description of the two explorers! Alas, the wickedness—if that's what it was—had been recorded.

There are many varieties of cigars for women—light, different in length, weight, leaf, and they are available in all the good brands. I am, in general, opposed to the cigarillo because I find it too heavy and often bitter, but favorably disposed to the Demi-tasse or Young Ladies or other miniature Havanas that match the larger versions in quality.

CARRYING A CIGAR

The best way is certainly the cigar case. It ought to be suited to the number you wish to carry, rigid, and made of leather that does not have an odor. To place a cigar in a coat pocket without protection is certainly to take a great risk. The wrapper, made from very thin, fine leaves, is able to deteriorate. If the wrapper is shredded, the cigar is completely lost! To avoid this, some manufacturers have wrapped each cigar in cellophane regardless of whether or not the cigars are boxed. True cigar fanciers distrust this practice—a recent one—because the wrapping may hide imperfections in the wrapper and it does not allow the cigar to "breathe," to mellow.

This is the same criticism leveled at the metal cigar case, use of which is increasing. My friend Dunhill, in London, affirms that a Havana in a metal container matures just as well as the naked Havana in a box. I disagree; a Havana ought to live, to breathe. It is plain that any wrapping (transparent paper or thin metal) stifles and places an obstacle in the way of the slow and subtle work of maturation.

A last bit of advice on this subject: never open a new box of cigars without having taken several precautions. Start by "reading" the box to learn as much as you can about the insides. Sometimes the date of shipment may be found. The famous green band, the seal of the Cuban government, is the assurance of proper manufacture, brand, and authenticity.

Look out for frauds—they are numerous. It is amusing to search for the signature—often in baroque lettering—of the proprietor of the plantation and the more modest stamp of the importer. A beautiful box of Havanas is a work of art. It has a right to respect and admiration. On the boxes of Rafael Gonzales (one of the better brands) you can read the following veritable profession of faith written in antiquated English script: "These cigars have been made from a secret blend of pure tobaccos from the Vuelta Abajo, selected by the Marqués Rafael Gonzales, grandee of Spain."

Each maker has his own symbol, decoration, exterior and interior colors, his own feeling. Use a special tool, which you can buy from a cigar merchant, to open the box. This tool has a short, flat blade that exerts strong pressure but will not endanger the cigars inside. Whether in a box, case, in your hand or mouth, treat your cigar with care. Your pleasure depends on it.

PART TWO

Choosing a Cigar

"What kind of cigar should I choose, Monsieur Davidoff? Please advise me."

"What sort of man are you? You cannot choose a cigar like a tie or a mystery story. I can only say that the best—Coronas, Panatelas, Perfectos, the three great types of cigars—are now in stock. You'll have to decide for yourself."

The moment of choosing a cigar is an important, difficult, and decisive one. Whether you are in the home of friends or in a cigar store stocking the latest Havana cigars, your decision should be weighed intelligently and according to the situation in which you find yourself. Never should the choice be an offhand matter. A cigar ought always to be an event. And I have only disdain for cigar chain-smoking. This practice may add to sales, but it vulgarizes the product.

Before choosing a cigar, think a moment. What will suit your mood? Don't forget, a cigar is a companion, and a rare one that will never slip away. You can call upon it at any time. But different cigars suit different circumstances or situations. Above all, take your time after a meal. Wait five or ten minutes, a quarter of an hour before lighting up. Outdoors, you can smoke the small, special cigars, those for sportsmen, hunters, golfers. It is not necessary to let the breeze smoke the cigar for you.

I was disturbed one day when one of my excellent clients, who had chosen a Corona, lighted it and declared:

"I am going to smoke it on the street."

"What a shame," I said. "You will waste the best of its pleasure."

He left in a fury. Nevertheless, he returned to the store because he knew I was right. A cigar cannot be truly enjoyed without contemplation, without thinking. You cannot smoke anything at any time, in any place. A cigar should fit your mood, habits, personality, surroundings. You can smoke dark, heavy cigars or light, green ones. Some people say that a man should choose a cigar that fits his physiognomy, avoiding cigars that are too long

29

or thin if he has a round face and cigars that are too short if he has a long face. "The cigar, like the pipe, ought to match your physique," wrote the painter Van Dongen.

It is necessary to take account of the gastronomic factor. No one should smoke after a light meal the same cigar he would after a meal full of heavy food and full-bodied wines. Never smoke immediately after a meal. A cigar is chosen to prolong the pleasant feeling of a good meal, of a fine wine, and should not be mixed with other flavors. The pleasures of the cigar are complementary. But they must be taken separately. In a work of Dorothy Sayers, Bunter, the valet of Lord Peter, pronounced this disdainful judgment: "This person is far from being a connoisseur: While drinking port, he smoked a Villar y Villar from your Grace's supply."

There is an occasion for each cigar and a cigar for each occasion. Maurice des Ombiaux advises not smoking a cigar "when hunting bears, the wolf, and the wild boar," because the odor might frighten away the beasts. He understands, quite correctly, that—after hunting—the fragrance of black and other strong-bodied cigars will harmonize well with the lingering "sweet odor of the dead leaves" trampled underfoot during the preceding hours.

Such subtle studies of the essence of cigars ought to be left to individual initiative. Every real cigar smoker has his own idiosyncrasies. He is attached to certain brands and to certain types of cigars. There are more than a thousand varieties of the Havana, each having a different strength, shape, and form. To discuss the merits of one cigar over another is part of the pleasure. There are, however, general rules to be followed during the average smoker's day.

THE MORNING

Contrary to the advice given by the celebrated Mexican bandit Pancho Villa to his men, do not smoke a cigar before breakfast. If, around eleven o'clock, after smoking several cigarettes, you

CHOOSING A CIGAR

have a strong need for a cigar, I suggest that you choose a light Havana. You might smoke, for example, a short one, a Panatela, which you can smoke quickly and which does not upset the delicate taste buds of the mouth. (Such cigars as these are especially good for women at any time of the day).

You might also smoke before lunch—without expecting too much satisfaction—a small Brazilian cigar (Suerdick, for example), a small Jamaican one (in general rather tasteless), or one from the Philippines, Mexico, or the Canary Islands.

During the morning you have the right to amuse yourself with the small, superficial pleasures, the *mini-voluptés,* to employ a phrase popular in France today. Of this sort are the small European cigars (Dutch, Belgian, or German) made, in general, with Indonesian, Borneo, or Sumatran tobacco. These cigars are not to be forgotten, although sometimes you may find them tasteless, stale, or even too strong!

From this "morning" list I have categorically omitted Indian cigars, which I find absolutely unsmokable, and American cigars. The latter have insides that are treated, debased, mashed into indefinable mixtures intended to give off exotic aromas. They are a humiliating form of candy for adults. In the morning, a smoker ought to "practice his scales" as does a pianist. The smoker awakens his taste but does not distort or neutralize it with a tobacco that is too strong.

A general rule: Be especially good to your taste buds in the morning. They will be grateful to you later.

AFTER LUNCH

Cigars of midday, those that suit the noon meal, ought to be chosen accordingly. I can never insist enough on this relationship between the meal and the cigar that caps it off. If the meal was one with meat and sauces, then the Havana you choose should be a heavy, long, full-bodied one. With a medium-weight meal, choose a medium-weight cigar. With a light lunch, a light cigar.

Do not light one cigar after another. As I mentined before, a

31

Havana should be smoked slowly and with dignity. A cigar in the middle of the day should not obliterate your faculties, your capacity to work. Especially during the work week, make sure that the cigar is not *too* heavy. The *claro* and the *colorado* (see the table of strengths, pages 38–39) are admirably suited to this noon period.

AFTERNOON

I have already said that I disapprove of chain-smoking cigars. The smoker must be at all times the master of his desires, his pleasures, and his nerves.

If the taste for tobacco sometimes frustrates you during the afternoon, smoke several small, light cigars or cigarillos. You should not smoke more than two or three medium-sized Havanas in the time between lunch and dinner.

Be careful—too much smoking will destroy your ability to taste, smell, to discriminate. For women who smoke at teatime, there are small cigars of an exquisite savor.

Do not smoke a cigar when working. If you do, you will smoke badly—and what is worse? You will smoke badly when writing, when thinking of something else. The cigar is exacting. It gives its all only to those who are consecrated to it, body and soul. Such an expression is not too strong.

During the afternoon, then, as in the morning, a small cigar is best. Choose one that is light, short, and not too strong. If you go outside, smoke one of the special cigars I have mentioned— Cazadores or Brevos. They are good for hunting, sports, or simply when taking a walk.

Patience. The evening—the time to enjoy a cigar fully—is drawing near.

AFTER DINNER

After a good meal filled with delicate tastes and assorted pleasures, prolonged with an after-dinner drink or simply strong coffee, the time to enjoy a Havana has arrived.

CHOOSING A CIGAR

I mean *a* Havana and not *several* Havanas. A cigar ought to last—to live—for around an hour. If you allow fifteen minutes after dinner, and another fifteen minutes after the first cigar is finished, time for lighting a second will come an hour and a half after finishing dinner; that is to say, when the conversation begins to flag.

If you dine early or plan ahead to smoke several cigars after dinner, it is best to move progressively from one strength and quality to another. As with wine or cheese, choose a stronger cigar after a lighter one, one less charged with tars.

Rule: A cigar that follows another should be greater in strength than the first.

But, once again, do not rush things. There is no greater pleasure than to sit down after dinner with a Havana. "The day has been difficult or pleasant or lyrical or savage. The man has fought, loved, and perhaps suffered. The weight of all the day's events and decisions is on his shoulders, and, with it, the consequences. These he may now measure or conjecture about. But he may also, for a moment, return to himself, return to his own contemplation. The blue smoke of a well-chosen cigar disappears into the air, a symbol, perhaps, of the vanity and precariousness of all things. No other object or person is capable of giving him such an opportunity to indulge in introspection, to contemplate his own being which is of such little significance in relation to the greater Being."

This passage from the work of Robert T. Lewis, a devoted cigar smoker who wrote several books on botany and geology in New Orleans at the end of the nineteenth century, well expresses the pleasure that awaits one with a cigar after dinner.

The cigar chosen should be one that fits the situation, that looks just right in the box or humidor, the cigar you have lovingly searched for and impatiently awaited. If you are a guest, ask your host's advice. With pleasure he will describe the condition of his cigars and may even suggest a sort of smoking "program" for the evening: perhaps a light-colored cigar of medium

33

length first, a *colorado;* a darker and larger, such as a demi-Corona, after.

You can always smoke one similar cigar after another. I do not say "identical," because no two cigars are alike. But never smoke a light Havana after one that is stronger. Most cigar smokers apply this rule instinctively.

STRENGTH OF THE CIGAR

The strength of a cigar is indicated by its color.

Rule: The darker the cigar, the stronger the taste. A good smoker ought to be able to estimate the strength of a cigar by the color of the wrapper and the visible part of the filler.

The best Havana companies use, in general, the same tobacco, but it has different nuances. Treatment of the leaf, its fermentation, and so on bring about different colors, and produce varying odors. But there are some more naturally colored tobaccos stronger than the others, and because of this they are termed *sur pied.*

At the beginning of this century, the Austro-Hungarian royal manufacturer of tobacco treated imported leaves with special care and offered in his catalogue more than 150 different nuances. The "palette" of the Havana is, in effect, of striking richness. The painter Auguste Renoir searched for special brown colors among the *colorados!* Today, to simplify things, the classification of colors has been greatly reduced. For several years, the taste (especially of American smokers) seems to be oriented toward the light cigars, *double claro,* almost blond, and the *claro,* nearly green. This type of cigar is erroneously called "fresh." It does have the advantage of being light, easy to smoke under all circumstances, adaptable to all situations, and is easily tolerated by women who do not smoke.

Certain of my smoker friends protest this trend: for them, the only true Havanas are those that have a dark look—the *colorados* or *maduros.* However, the "light" smokers regard those who smoke strong cigars with inquietude and reprobation. They believe that the heavy, dark cigars depress the spirit, burn the mouth, brutalize the taste buds, transport a strong nicotine odor. Neither group is correct.

If dark cigars will always be considered the greatest (like great wines, which dominate the table), you can also discover some great light-colored ones that have matured for at least eight months but not more than a year. It is not true that a darker cigar has more nicotine than a lighter one. It is, I have found, sometimes the opposite. The inside of a green cigar is darker than the wrapper, which has been effected by a special method of maturing and fermentation. It is also necessary to clear up one error that confounds many smokers: thinking that the green cigar is a fresh one. A green cigar is not a fresh cigar but simply a light-colored one. Its color is obtained today by a special treatment of the plant. The plant is protected from the rays of the sun, and the chlorophyl is retained in the picking (charcoal process).

The assumption undoubtedly can be made that the light-colored cigar does not age as well as one better suited to maturation. It dries more easily. It ought to be smoked at an earlier stage in order to compensate for the lack of maturity and body of the wrapper.

In broader terms, the producers get the *double claro* by picking the leaf before it has reached maturity. Its pallor comes from a rapid drying process, sometimes under a wood fire or from candles, *capa chandella*. The *double claro,* which requires so much care, is very delicate and hard to find. It is, I feel, much less satisfying than a better-aged cigar. So far as the *claro* is concerned, the leaf picked before maturity is dried rapidly in the open air. (In fermenting a *colorado claro,* a darker nuance is sought.) But late picking or slower fermentation does not suffice to explain the color of the tobacco and its strength. In certain cases, the position of the leaves determines the color. The *maduro*

—dark tobacco—is often found among the highest leaves, where it is exposed to especially strong sunlight. Its fermentation is prolonged. The *oscuro*, even darker-leaf tobacco, is subjected to an even longer fermentation period.

This problem is not a simple one, and colors are as diverse as concepts. Each important maker has his own standards, and the term *claro*, for example, is not considered a standard *per se* but simply an easy way of designating a shade and strength by a particular manufacturer. That understood, look at the following chart. It is all theory, mind you, but it may help you choose a Havana according to its shade.

	COLOR	REMARKS
Oscuro	black	Very strong taste; very little aroma; not popular. This cigar was very much in fashion at the beginning of the century.
Maduro	brown-black	Strong; suits smokers of experience.
Maduro colorado	brown	Of medium strength; somewhat more aromatic than the maduro.
Colorado	reddish-brown	As full-bodied as the preceding three but more aromatic.
Colorado claro	light brown	A little lighter than the colorado.
Claro	tobacco brown	The most popular of the mild cigars because of the fineness of its aroma. It is the easiest cigar to smoke.

CHOOSING A CIGAR

Double claro or *Clarissimo* or *Claro-claro*	green	Very mild; especially popular in the United States. This cigar is gaining in popularity everywhere.

Each famous maker produces his own specialties, and nuances exist in every variety. Special tobaccos vary from year to year. It would be vain to attempt a qualitative table that would list the great producers in each category. It is better to seek information regularly and adapt your "purchase policy" to the information received.

THE FORM OF THE CIGAR

To describe a cigar is a delicate task that requires a certain number of skills: you have to indicate the brand, then the type (or standard size), and finally the coloration. Types may exist in different strengths (even those of the same brand). For example: I can smoke an excellent Cabanas (brand) Panatela (type or model) *colorado* (color/strength). If you can handle all this terminology, you are a true connoisseur and all smokers will respect your judgment.

There have been on the market many types of cigars that have disappeared. Some have been (and still are) created exclusively for certain merchants. Only an expert can say with certainty when a cigar was put on the market for sale and when such types as the following became popular: Alvas, Aromans, Cedros, Divinos, Eminentes, Invincibles, Principes, Barones, Czares, Patriotas, Salamones.

It is easy to get lost in the Havana directories. Actually, the lover of cigars can afford to forget about the lost specimens of the past. He should be acquainted with the rough outline of cigar history. The record varies as to color, length, and circumference according to the various catalogues, but certain forms remain

37

constant. One pointer: don't confuse the term *Corona*, which describes the most popular shape, with the brand name Corona.

	HEAD	BODY	FOOT
Corona symbol C	Rounded, closed	Straight, parallel sides	cut
Perfecto symbol P	Half-pointed, closed	Cylindrical in form; it tapers toward the foot and toward the head according to the type	full-pointed or truncated
Panatela symbol PN	Rounded, open	Straight, parallel sides; tapering	cut
Lonsdale symbol L	Rounded, closed	Straight, parallel sides; slimmer than the Corona; thicker than the Panatela	cut
Culebras (snake) symbol CB	closed	Flat, braided; three cigars together, twisted and overlapping	cut
Demi-tasse symbol DT	Rounded, closed	Straight, regular; a Corona of small dimensions	cut

The table, of course, gives nothing more than a summary of shapes. It does remind me of several things, however: the Corona shape (rounded head, foot cut) is the classic shape and the most common one. Yet in this category, as in all others, there are an endless variety of lengths, strengths, and other differences. The Perfecto shape is disappearing. The Torpedo (fat, pot-bellied, closed at both ends) has almost disappeared. It still has some fervent fans. "Nothing will ever replace the Torpedo," wrote Charles Graves recently in his *Rich Man's Little Guide;* "nothing will replace this pleasure. Its fat belly gives the most refreshing smoke."

It is the youthful-looking Panatela—as opposed to the paunchy Torpedo—which is *à la mode* now. The Panatela's sales increase from year to year, and all the larger makers list it in their catalogues. It is the newest cigar, the trimmest.

Which shape should you choose? Each to his own taste, to be sure. Remember only that the Torpedo has virtually disappeared, the Corona shape is the most common, the Perfecto loses popularity, and the Panatela gains. From the viewpoint of pleasure, there is no real difference. It is wrong to pretend that the Perfecto holds more of the aroma because its foot is not cut. The Panatela, a finer cigar, smokes more rapidly than the Corona, but its market is expanding. In the matter of cigars, fashion changes quickly.

SIZE OF THE CIGAR

There are cigars of all sizes, of all lengths. The circumference often increases with the length of the cigar, but this is not a rule. There are some very fat small cigars and some very thin long ones. The average, classic shape is the Corona, which measures between five and a half and six inches in length. The measurement of a cigar is established by custom. Any measurement taken to mean the standard or classic is an artificial one as any company can put a cigar of a different size on the market.

To my knowledge, the smallest Havana ever manufactured is a Corona of Bolívar, called the Delgado, which does not measure more than one inch and a quarter. The longest, except for a Panatela measuring nineteen and a half inches, is a cigar called the Koh-I-Noor. It was manufactured before World War II by Henry Clay for a maharajah. A grotesque cigar six feet two inches long, it is to be found in the Tobacco Museum in Bunde,

West Germany. I do advise avoiding cigars that are too short or too long. In this domain, as well, the size and proportion are the mark of a man of good taste.

Each manufacturer is his own master in the matter of size and is free to introduce any size he wants at any time. Some clients have special cigars "made to measure." They want to be the only ones smoking a particular shape or length. From the smallest to the largest cigar, we proceed to the ladder of the classic and standard sizes.

SMALL CORONAS

With a length of one and a half inches, the Delgado de Bolívar (a small Corona) is the smallest of the current cigars. Specially made by the Bolívar firm (which has other fine products), this cigarillo is convenient for women and for those who have trouble with too much smoking. A Delgado ought to last at least a half-hour and to give a great deal of pleasure.

DEMI-TASSE

An inch or an inch and a half longer than the small Coronas, these are also called Young Ladies or Lady Finger. It is an easy cigar to carry, convenient to smoke, and can be found in all nuances—from *double claro* to the *colorado*. Personally, I enjoy the Demi-tasse *claros* of Rey del Mundo and those of Rafael Gonzales, but you can find other good types among all the good Havana brands.

SMALL PANATELA

Following this theoretical classification, you come next to the small Panatelas, which are around four and a half inches long, but because of their lightness (they are the thinnest of the Panatelas) they are grouped after the Demi-tasse.

Fanciers of small Panatelas can today find their type in almost any brand. For my part, I most often select the small Panatelas of

CHOOSING A CIGAR

Partagas (called the Delgados Chicas), those of Rafael Gonzales (Epicures), and those of the Punch brand.

PANATELA

It measures from four and a half to five inches, but is thicker than its cousin the small Panatela. It offers more of the characteristics of the true cigar, and its satisfactions.

What Panatelas to consider? Considering the crops, the years, the tastes, and chance, the best in general include those of Rafael Gonzales, Upmann, Romeo y Julieta, Belinda, Bolívar, and Rey del Mundo.

DEMI-CORONA

We now leave the province of the small cigars, smoked by both women and men, popular because of lightness, fine lines, and mildness rather than body—using an expression common to connoisseurs of great wines and cigar fanciers. With the demi-Corona, we reach the domain of serious, true cigars, measuring no more than two and a half to three inches—that is to say, less than a Panatela but thick enough in diameter so that the true smoker is able to draw pleasure from it.

The demi-Corona is the smallest of the large cigars. You can find them of all different sorts. The best, to my taste, are the Château Haut-Brion from Hoyo de Monterrey (a Davidoff creation: I hold the exclusive rights), the Punch No. 3, Montecristo No. 5, Ramón Allones No. 3. I would also mention, without giving any particulars, the demi-Coronas of Partagas and Upmann among those excellent cigars that Cuba puts on the market each year.

LITTLE CORONA

A little larger than the demi-Corona (around three inches), the little Corona is an ideal cigar for the afternoon. It is also good after a light lunch if you choose a light, pale one. A coarser, darker little Corona finishes off a dinner if you are, for example, in a hurry to get to the theater.

In this category I put the accent on the Château-Laffitte, a specialty of mine, on the Montecristo No. 4, and the Partagas No. 4. Bolívar, Upmann, and Punch also produce some excellent little Coronas in their range from light to coarse.

CORONAS

The Corona is the king of cigars. Its five and one-quarter inches in length constitutes the ideal size. Its diameter is so calculated that the flow of smoke is perfect. It embodies all that is necessary for the connoisseur—the perfume, the aroma, the essential vapors. All the major makers have always sought to produce the best Coronas, and they exist in all types. In spite of the current vogue for Panatelas, the Coronas account for the largest part of all cigar sales. For many years, knowing that this is *the* cigar, some smokers did not even try other cigars without fear, since they were sure that the best leaves were saved for the Coronas. It is a different situation today. But the legend holds, and many cigar fanciers will refuse a Panatela or a Demi-tasse, convinced as they are that the tobacco is inferior.

The good Coronas are numerous. I recommend Château Margaux and Château-Latour (Hoyo de Monterrey and Davidoff), super-selection of Punch, Montecristo No. 3, Ramón Allones No. 1, Romeo y Julieta Cedros No. 2. . . . This list is not exhaustive. Each man has the right (and the duty) to defend his favorite Corona.

LONSDALE

The Lonsdale is an imperious cigar (six to six and a half inches), and is marvelously adapted to great dinners, elegant evenings. It is, especially in the *maduro* and *colorado* strengths and colors, the cigar of the VIP, and—for him—a must. The Lonsdale gives to the smoker the maximum of pleasure, a quantity of abundant, fragrant smoke. Among the good Lonsdales I would point out Château-Yquem (Davidoff), Punch No. 7, Montecristo No. 2 (which has a peculiar pointed shape), and the Lonsdale of Rafael Gonzales.

DOUBLE CORONA

Sometimes termed a "chair rung," this super cigar varies in size from eight to nine inches. It is often associated with those men who are searching for a special effect, or possess the complex of a tycoon, of little Caesars. It is also the cigar that is held in the mouth the most and which gives off the heaviest odor. Edward VII, Churchill, and Farouk were great fans of the double Corona. Some smokers consider them indispensable when they are seated behind a gambling table or in a night club. It is true that the size harmonizes well with a champagne bucket.

In this super category I would point out the Clemenceaus, the Churchill of Romeo y Julieta; the double Corona of Punch, of Upmann, of Hoyo de Monterrey, of Rey del Mundo; and the Bernardo of Partages. Dark and strong tobaccos, one can understand, are used more often than the *claros*.

OTHER SHAPES

In the preceding pages we have not mentioned more than the types of cigars regularly produced by Havana makers and which, in general, set the standards for cigar manufacture in the rest of the world. But this list should not limit anyone. Nothing should prevent the connoisseur from requesting a cigar maker to produce an original cigar—of any form—with an original band and name. There are numerous ephemeral shapes to be found in every variety—*fabulosos, microscópicos, inmensos*—which have come and gone.

PRECAUTIONS IN BUYING

When you purchase any sort of cigars made by an established

manufacturer and buy them from a reputable merchant, your chances are excellent that they will be in perfect shape when you open the box. Accidents may have happened along the way, however, in which case you should ask for an explanation and an exchange from the seller.

1. Stained cigar: little stains of mildew on the wrapper, which are not to be confused with the drops produced by the summer months' fermentation. The mildew may not be serious, but in any case consult your merchant. You may also see small spots of discoloration: they will not affect in any way the quality of the cigar.

2. Wrapper undone: the cigar has been exposed to too much dryness. It has traveled too long (the cigar sometimes has seasickness) or was left exposed for too long without adequate humidity.

3. Cigar too humid: it is mushy; difficult, if not impossible, to light.

4. Wrapper shows traces of plant ribs, veins: this is evidence that the leaf used for the wrapper was not the very best—that is to say, it was cut from lower down on the plant.

When one is protected by the mark of a good manufacturer, there is little chance of such unpleasant surprises.

THE GREAT NAMES

When Fidel Castro rose to power, one of his first gestures was to nationalize sugar and cigars, the two principal resources of Cuba. During the fever of the revolution, Castro decided that the epoch of great cigars was over and that the baroque decor of the packaging (gold and purple) was an anomaly. Accordingly, declared the chief of the *Barbudos,* such cigars would no longer be manufactured (960 existing varieties). In place would be a single cigar for the populace (in three or four varieties at the maximum). With the great names, the best Havanas—vestiges of decadent capitalism and the power of money—were condemned without appeal.

CHOOSING A CIGAR

As you can imagine, I followed these events from Geneva with great interest. I felt that the Havana would triumph in time, but I did not think that victory would come so quickly.

Several months later two emissaries of the Cuban revolutionary government arrived at my shop. In essence, they asked: "Monsieur Davidoff, What are we to do? No one is buying our cigars. The sales keep getting lower."

They proposed a meeting with me and the directors of Cubatabaco. Several meetings followed in which the problem was debated and I tried to explain that the richness of Cuba—in the matter of cigars—was to be found in diversity. If Castro did not maintain the tradition, he would ruin the market, perhaps forever. The Cubans finally adopted my view, although they later created a popular cigar, the Siboney, which still exists but has had no international success.

The great Cuban brands, thought to be souvenirs, were alive again! There were many difficulties. Dispossessed proprietors had rebelled against their treatment; some of them sued for action in the World Court at the Hague. Others left Cuba and established businesses elsewhere—in Virginia, Florida, the Philippines, in the Canary Islands, in the Middle East. This was the case with the Henry Clay, Corona, Cabanas, and Murias companies, whose cigars today are on the market but are no longer Havanas.

Numerous rumors circulated. It was claimed that certain proprietors had removed their best plants for planting in other lands; that the best workers had followed them; that they had destroyed the best of the plantations in leaving Cuba; that the sacred square of Vuelta Abajo would never again produce tobacco of fine quality. Some believed the secrets of cultivation had been transported with the exiles.

Today the great brand names are the property of the Cuban people: Partagas, Larranaga, Hoyo de Monterrey, Upmann, Rafael Gonzales, Romeo y Julieta, Bock, Allones, Punch, Montecristo, and the like. Cigars are produced under national standards

45

and their quality is easily as high as those of cigars produced in the pre-Castro period. Sometimes they are better, since the cultivation in certain areas has been improved. For true cigar smokers, there is still the same excellent selection to choose from.

There are smokers who claim to be able—blindfolded—to identify the maker of a cigar if you give them the year of manufacture. Similarly, if you give them the name of the maker, they will identify the year. Even more strange is the following case. Three Spaniards, unknown to me, absolutely confounded me one day at my shop in Geneva.

"Show us," one of them said, "your very best Havanas."

I opened several boxes. They smoked for a while in silence. Each took a different selection. Then the first, opening his eyes, said:

"Cape de Vinales, tobacco of Palicios."

The second: "Cape de Vinales, tobacco of San Luis."

And the third: "Cape d'Isabel María, tobacco of the Semi Vuelta."

That had been all. They left enchanted after having purchased several boxes. I never saw them again. But the certainty of their identification struck me so forcefully that on a trip to Cuba, I checked them out. They were not mistaken. Never had I met such connoisseurs. There probably aren't any others quite so expert.

This anecdote gives an idea of the degree of sensibility that can be attained. Recognizing the plantation from which the fermented leaf had been gathered is a miracle. But to know how to identify a good cigar, one made by an expert, is the work of all enlightened smokers. I turn to several different *fincas* each year for the filler of my Châteaux. I am not certain which one or group of plantations has produced the leaf, but all of them are within the limits of the Vuelta Abajo.

Tobacco leaf is cultivated in a large part of Cuba. But the region that produces the best leaf is the Vuelta Abajo in the province of Piñar del Río. Each *vega* of the Vuelta has its own character. The leaves most sought after come from the communes of San Luis and San Juan y Martinez where the soil (an important detail) is sandy. Each year the Vuelta Abajo produces 21,000 tons of tobacco leaf—approximately forty per cent of the total production in Cuba. It is the birthplace of the great tobaccos, the best cigars. Vuelta Abajo is a name every smoker should know. To the east of the Vuelta Abajo, in the Semi Vuelta, a somewhat heavier leaf is produced; it does not have the bouquet of the Vuelta Abajo.

The other important regions are Partido (red soil), Remedios (in the center of the island), and the East, but their production is much inferior in quality.

The smoker can choose any of the great Havana brands cited in this text without fear. He is in royal terrain, that of Vuelta Abajo. He risks nothing. Sooner or later he will choose one brand or another and stay with this because of habit or familiarity.

PHILOSOPHY OF CHOICE

The choice of a cigar is not a simple thing, as all the preceding remarks and tables have made clear. There are an infinite number of combinations and possibilities. Some of my clients, both the celebrated and the unknown, are fixed for all time on one or two varieties and will not be convinced to try anything new. My Châteaux have attracted some faithful clients: Prince Rainier chooses the Château-Margaux and the Rafael Gonzales; Darryl Zanuck is attracted by the Coronas of Rey del Mundo; ex-Prime Minister of France Antoine Pinay regularly orders the Château-Yquem.

I have other clients who often change their brand, their model. For them, and for others, I have in reserve in Geneva, in Zurich, and in my air-conditioned caves at the free port of Basel, a million and a half cigars that are resting or "working." The clients can really make a choice. In fact, while the choice does vary a bit, it is usually the same with regard to color (that is, strength) and shape.

All of this is, to say the least, a matter of taste. What is most important is to be sure of your taste. You can understand now why my response to the usual question, "Monsieur Davidoff, what do you suggest?" is always so evasive. After all, you select according to color, shape, brand name, and eventually you will be attracted to one or two cigars that seem right. If you are a beginner or an occasional smoker, you will probably stay with the fine cigars, the light ones, the Panatela for example. Later, you might want to make the acquaintance of heavier cigars, thicker and longer ones. If you smoke too much already, you should not choose a cigar of more than four inches. If you are a man who smokes one cigar a day (or two), a Havana of five inches (a Corona perhaps) is perfect. If you are very sensitive to smoke, you should stay with light cigars. If you are a heavy smoker and your taste buds are already conditioned, you can choose a *maduro*, heavy, fragrant, musky. If you are a woman. . . .

In the midst of all these *ifs* is one sure thing: whatever your tastes, your habits, your needs, there is a cigar which will be right, one that is adapted to your constitution, which harmonizes with your mood.

There is no more faithful servant or companion than a Havana. To learn to choose a cigar which is right for you is to exercise your talent for self-awareness. To find the cigar which suits you is a particular joy. In *Gigi* by Colette, Aunt Alice, the depository of all female intellect, tells a docile student: "Allow me to dream of teaching you how to choose cigars. . . . When a woman knows the preferences of a man, cigars included, and when a man knows what pleases a woman, they are well armed for their life together."

A well-chosen cigar is like armor and is useful against the torments of life. A little blue smoke mysteriously removes anxiety.

48

PART THREE

Keeping
Your
Cigars

Choosing a cigar is a complicated and subjective art. Many different factors enter into the decision. But above all, it is imperative to choose (and this is not subjective) a cigar in good condition. That is to say, one that is not too humid, too dry, too young, or too old. Never choose one that is fermenting.

A Havana has a life of its own. It "matures." Once a year during the early period of its life, it will exude some oil if properly humidified. One day Paderewski told me that when a violinist plucked certain strings of his Stradivarius, all the Stradivari in the surrounding area vibrated in their cases. In the period corresponding to the Cuban summer, Havanas everywhere in the world, kept under the right conditions, ferment together. During the first years, fine drops of oil (which some call the "flower" of the cigar) are deposited on the tip. A very light perfume, sweetly enervating, spreads through the cellars where the Havanas are stored. The fermentation is much less noticeable after the third year, and you must have an excellent sense of smell and good eyesight to detect it. Like a vintage wine, the cigar attains its state of perfection and rests there for some time before declining and slowly losing its bouquet.

Many stupid things have been written about the ripening and conserving of the Havana cigar, its "life" in the box, its aging and changes, the necessity of humidifying.

Rule: Each kind of Havana possesses its own laws of conservation and its rhythms of development and decline. Usually, a good Havana will keep its quality for fifteen years. It is not the same cigar, however, when first stored, as it is three years later, or after ten years in storage. You can choose between a fresh cigar, one that has matured a bit, or an ancient one. Each epoch of the Havana has its own special pleasure, and each step in itself is a great one.

The fifteen-year rule is nevertheless not an absolute one. While making a trip to Cuba in search of fine tobacco, I found myself one day on a small farm (*finca*) and was welcomed by the modest planter. Since I had bought some high-quality leaves, the farmer decided to give me some Villar y Villars dating from the time of his grandfather. I accepted them without enthusiasm because they seemed too old. But the head of the family, seeing my reluctance, gave me a nod of encouragement. I lighted one of the cigars; it was excellent. To the usual aroma of the brand was added an unidentifiable and subtle perfume, a note of sadness, a subtle resonance—perhaps a mark of the time from which they dated. Astonished, I asked when the cigars were made.

"1911," he told me. "A great year. . . ."

It was true. And more than a quarter of a century old.

"Come see," said the farmer, "where we store our cigars so that they do not lose any quality."

He led me to a simple, old and thick wooden chest, slightly worm-eaten, which was placed in a slightly humid cellar. It reminded me of the old caves of provincial France where the delicate liquors age and become charged with body. In any case, it was proof that a Havana is of good stock. If it is treated well, it can defy time itself!

Of course, what is possible in Cuba—a humid climate and one perfect for tobacco—is not always possible in Europe or North America. By the time the cigars have reached these regions, they may have suffered from the transportation. You cannot keep a cigar there for twenty-five years, even if it is a good vintage given the very best of care.

But you can keep a cigar ten, twelve, fifteen years and get the same pleasure from it. All this depends on how you keep it "alive."

THE PLANT

In order to practice the simple laws for guarding the quality of cigars in the home, it is useful to have some ideas about the

52

leaf, its maturation, the different ways of fermenting it, and the manufacture of the cigar. There are many legends. Who has not heard of the beautiful cigar girls with burning eyes who roll the most beautiful cigars along their naked thighs? These ladies are not creatures of legend. They do exist—in diminishing numbers. I shall introduce them later.

Growing the leaf is a difficult and minute enterprise. The Cuban prepares his ground several months before the sowing time and lives solely for tobacco, "without a fixed hour to start his day or to terminate it." This line is a quotation from Gaspar Jorge García Gallo, a former tobacco worker with Upmann and Romeo y Julieta.

The tobacco leaf does not need much water. The morning dew and several good rain showers are sufficient for its development. The oldest text I know of about tobaccos is a letter written by Demetrio Pela, originally from the Canary Islands and one of the first Cuban immigrants who, soon after the Spanish Conquest, questioned the Indians about cultivation. I even know the name of the person who gave him the secrets—an Indian, Erioxil Panduca, who became his associate in business. By the virtue of the gods, declared Panduca, tobacco does not need more than two rains per month. An excess of water will steal its honey.

The firm Pela and Panduca, founded around 1600, had not more than a theoretical existence. One can imagine the small planting fields arranged around pioneers' cabins and along the rivers, as well as the confusion which must have prevailed when time came to cut and treat the leaf. What were the products of this activity? One can only guess, because not until 1614 did the Spanish crown authorize the cultivation of tobacco and define "smoking tobacco" as the aim of all this activity.

In the beginning, drying was an open-air process. Next, the leaf was roughly rolled and bound to others with the aid of a thread. Things are much different today. Leaves undergo a series

53

of treatments or cures which vary according to the origin of the leaf, its quality, and its eventual use. The tobacco for wrappers of fine cigars is not treated the same way as filler tobacco; nor is that sold overseas to make mediocre cigars—unjustly sold with a Havana label—treated in the same way.

The seed sprouts five to eight days after planting. The bedding of tobacco plants takes place between the thirty-fifth and fortieth day following planting of seed. About a month later the first signs of maturation appear. The leaves, which were a dull green, become lighter and more brilliant. They lose their bloom. The farmer closely examines the head of the plant and its ribs; this tells him whether it is ready for cutting. If he wishes to produce light tobacco—a *claro* cigar—he will cut the leaf prematurely. If he has orders for darker tobacco—*colorado, maduro*—he will wait several weeks. The time may come—especially when the rain has been more frequent than usual—when the farmer will be able, one or two months later, to obtain a second harvest of smaller, lesser-quality leaves, the *capadura*. But this seldom happens. Most often, the dryness is such that, in certain areas, the main harvest is the only one.

To walk down between columns of high, ripe, and heavy leaves before they are gathered is a great experience. The filtered sunlight is yellow and green—the light of an aquarium without water. Sometimes, certain young and special plants—eagerly awaited—are protected from the sun by netting. On the large plantations, formidable guards are posted to ferret out poachers. A walk through the immense green boulevards is a meditative one, dominated by the sun and silence, and an even perfume.

Gathered with care, the leaves are then dried. In general, the farmer gives up at this stage. He sells his leaves. Only the rich landlords control the operation from start to finish.

The leaves are stored in vast barns where they dry, losing water and starch. There are three kinds of drying, three kinds of "treatments." The most popular is air treatment; the leaves are simply hooked on crossbars in the barn—higher and higher up toward the roof (made of palm leaves or guano) as they lose their humidity. The air-drying process varies according to weather conditions. If the humidity is high, reaching eighty-five per cent, it will be necessary to expose the leaves to the sun before they begin to bulge. If the weather is too rainy, it will be necessary to light a charcoal fire in order to reduce the amount of moisture in the air. Sometimes the floor is watered or spread with damp cloths if dryness is the problem. The north windows—or, conversely, the south—are opened to let in the night moisture. You can understand why the most experienced engineers of these picturesque tobacco-curing barns have the right to the title Doctor.

Treatment by sunlight is reserved for tobacco taken from plants that are cut down in one piece. These are exposed on wooden trays around the drying barn or in the fields. They have to be watched constantly and immediately protected in case of rain. After several days, when the leaves have yellowed and matured, they are returned to the barn and the air cure follows. This mixed method is more and more popular, a little too rough, I feel. The sun "consumes" the tobacco and lightly burns the leaves.

The cure by fire is a relatively recent development. It comes from the customers' taste for *double claros* or *clarissimos*—the gray-green cigars which are more and more appreciated, especially in the United States, and which pass, mistakenly, as less charged with nicotine. The leaves are dried with artificial heat from a wood or charcoal fire. In the Vuelta Abajo this practice has been used for a dozen years. I have seen old planters with tears in their eyes saying, "It is a shame, sir." "The taste, the aroma, the elasticity of our tobacco will disappear . . . soon you will not be able to distinguish Cuban leaf tobacco from any imported variety!"

But the *clarissimo* is more and more in demand, drying by

wood fire gains more territory, and old farmers are quickly disappearing.

THE THREEFOLD FERMENTATION OF THE LEAF

Fermentation follows the drying. The leaves need to be freed of nitrogen and resins. After the drying process they are tied in bunches. This is done during humid weather in order to eliminate the risk of ripping the fragile leaf. The leaves are piled up on a bed of guano and banana-tree leaves. At the top of the pile one ought to be able to gauge the quality of the tobacco. If the year has been dry, the tobacco will be of good quality. The pile is high because the heat of fermenting leaf (dry leaf) ought to be intense. If the year has been rainy, the tobacco will be light; the pile is kept small because there is no need for anything except light fermentation at this stage.

The pile is covered on all sides by palm leaves or light cloths. In several days the temperature will have risen; the process of fermentation has begun. It should be watched carefully. If the heat rises too quickly, the leaves will deteriorate. In this case, the pile is pulled apart and divided into smaller ones. This first step in fermentation lasts around two months. The maximum temperature is reached after thirty days; following this, it lowers itself progressively. The tobacco becomes "light," ready for selection.

This is the first stage of fermentation. It won't be the last. In leaving the vast barn, the leaf leaves behind its first heating up. But it will be submitted to other treatments. And it will "live" until it reaches the lips of the smoker.

THE PRECIOUS LEAF

Dried, fermented, the tobacco leaf will be packed and sent to different warehouses. The whole village is ready for the operation of selecting leaves, and this procedure takes place in an air of festivity. The tobacco will be stored for twelve to eighteen months before being used.

The workers have prepared, from their own special recipes, a mixture that is placed at the bottom of each of the casks. They spray the leaves, then pack them in cases. They are removed the next day to make the selection, or classification. The leaves are divided into *capas* (wrapper leaf), the best ones, or *tripas* (filler leaf). But the process is not completed. In each category there are more than ten subcategories relating to thickness, color, texture, shape, and the like. It is at this point that the true connoisseur shows his cards. Those who have never visited these villages will always be ignorant of the true art of selecting tobacco.

Before the packing, a second stage of fermentation is undertaken. The leaves are put together in sheaves. Sometimes, when the fermentation process is too slow, the leaves are watered once again. The now-humid tobacco is placed between palm leaves in sheaves. It is in this form that they arrive at the factory "maturing" because the leaf keeps fermenting. The casks in the warehouse will be watched, rolled, and moved around in order to accomplish this second stage of fermentation evenly.

Now comes the manufacturing phase. The sheaves are extracted from their casks. You have to have a strong stomach to put up with the odor of fermentation at this stage. It is violent, penetrating, staggering. Again the workers water the bunches and then shake them dry. Then they put them in baskets where they spend the night before being delivered to the cutters.

These are the real glamour girls of the cigar. They have the legendary "naked thighs." They perpetuate the memory of Carmen and the girls of the tobacco factories of Seville who led such a relatively brief existence. Usually young, attractive girls with all shades of skin color from white to dark brown, gay and lively, they fill the immense workroom or "gallery," seated on little leather stools. Their work consists of removing the central rib of the leaf. Their job is to open the wet leaf on a small board held across their thighs, and to split the rib skillfully between their thumb and index finger. They perform this work with song and laughter.

The leaf is then put into a cask, mechanically pressed, and stored in a barn for a new period of fermentation, the third and sometimes the longest one. If the tobacco is heavy, juicy, and thick, it will stay for several years in storage, maturing. In certain cases, for up to ten years!

FROM THE LEAF TO THE CIGAR

You can understand the importance of the fermenting process —and the time devoted to it—when you consider the end product.

Another essential operation will take place after this third period of work: the mixing. The cigar's aroma depends on it. Accomplished specialists, experts in a particular type, have the important job of finding the same aroma year after year, thus assuring a continuity which is the mark of the great names in cigars. With a preoccupied air, they amble through the rooms where the leaves are suspended "like," Paul Morand has written, "pieces of silk from a dirigible." These inspectors and selectors "allow themselves to be guided by intuition."

Once the difficult mixture is made, the tobacco is lightly sprinkled and placed in casks where the aromatic melange is created. A delicate perfume rises when the casks are opened many months later for the first steps of manufacture. You are far away from the savage and brutal odor of the warehouse sheaves.

It is now that the cigarmaker enters the scene. Contrary to some opinion, and to the detriment of the legend, the maker is a qualified male worker, and, in general, an older man. He pulls the wrapper from its humid cloth, extends it on a board, stretches it out some more, and trims the edges. Next, he rolls the filler with great care, measures it, and places it in the wrapper. He has made what is called the "barrel." It remains for him to make the head and the foot and to attach the wrapper with a special gum. A cigar is made by hand, but it is not rolled on the thigh. It takes its shape on a small workbench with the precise gestures employed by a watchmaker. It is often said that Havana cigars are made, even now, by machine. This is not true for the best of them.

There are machines capable of replacing manual labor at all stages of the cigar's manufacture. Certain large American manufacturers have put into operation machines capable of selecting leaves for mixtures. More sensibly, machines can be used to separate, twist, roll, attach, and so on.

Only the making of cigarettes is mechanized in Cuba. The cigar is made by hand. (For the popular brands, filler may be made by machine.) The wrapper is too thin, too delicate to be treated by a machine in any reasonable state. But the threat of mechanization is always present, and I must admit that under modern economic conditions this threat is growing constantly.

In 1925 Por Larranaga imported from the United States to Cuba the first machine to make cigars. It was exhibited in the streets of Havana during working hours and the people came to admire the regularity of its production. But a protest movement got under way, strikes broke out, and Por Larranaga decided to return the machine.

From the consumer's viewpoint, is the quality of cigars produced by machines inferior to that of those produced by hand? The answer is an unqualified yes, and this even if all the preliminary operations (choice and the like) are done by hand. When mechanically selected, the leaf chosen for the wrapper will be thicker and rougher. I am thankful for the spirited reaction of the workers and hope that such feeling is long maintained. But for how much longer?

Already the atmosphere in the workrooms is not the same any more. Readers once recited verses (often those of Victor Hugo) or commented on the news of the day. This picturesque practice was born in the workrooms of Don Jaime Partagas around 1850. Despite the opposition of some anxious manufacturers, readings were held in all the factories by 1860. And, in the days that preceded the War of Cuban Independence, the factories were the stages of political agitation. Speeches being forbidden provoked a veritable uprising. You can safely say that the movement for the independence of Cuba, at the end of the nineteenth century, was born in the cigar factories. Now, on each of my trips, I notice that the radio is slowly replacing the reader. The first receiver was installed in 1923 in the Cabanas y Carbajol factory. It is true that there are still readers in some factories. Conferences have been held there. Castro did not neglect this opportunity for broadcasting his social gospel. But Victor Hugo is losing ground every day to modern music.

THE FRESH CIGAR

The last stages of manufacturing are no less full of poetry and picturesque detail. Before leaving the factory, the cigars are usually bound together with a silk ribbon in packets of fifty each. This packet is called a half-wheel. In Cuba a man who has reached the age of fifty is said to have reached his half-wheel. These are placed for several weeks in a cedar cabinet where they will "consume" the heat of the third stage of fermentation. They have to "take some air," and to lose a certain amount of humidity acquired during the different manufacturing processes. Another choice will be made a month later: the cigars are divided according to the color of the wrapper into fundamental categories—*claro, maduro,* and numerous secondary nuances which are different with each manufacturer.

After that the cigars are put in boxes, another delicate operation

Groucho Marx–the man who undoubtedly turned the unlit cigar into the world's most famous stage and screen prop. Offstage, Groucho chose strong Havanas.

Top left: Jack Benny mugging with cigar in a production of *Charlie's Aunt;* top right: Odette Myrtil impersonating George Sand, à la cigar, in a scene from *White Lilacs;* bottom: Groucho and cigar on the set of *Animal Crackers.*

Minnie Maddern Fiske, famed for her role in *Tess of the D'Urbervilles* during the 1890s, is here pictured doing her own long-hair takeoff of George Sand— walking stick and hat included.

Edward VII, whose mother, Queen Victoria, had banned the smoking of cigars in court. On the day Edward assumed the throne he announced to those attending him: "Gentlemen, you may smoke."

Winston Churchill, one of the world's most celebrated cigar smokers, reportedly smoked more than 300,000 cigars in his lifetime. When the German blitz destroyed the Dunhill shop in London, the manager rushed to the phone at two in the morning to inform Sir Winston that his private stock of cigars was safe.

Fiorello LaGuardia reaching for a match to light his cigar after a conference with President Roosevelt in 1938. LaGuardia often preferred leaving the cigar band on while smoking.

Ernst Lubitsch watching the rushes of *Trouble in Paradise* in 1932. Lubitsch smoked his cigars practically down to the stub.

During the war years Orson Welles gave hundreds of magic shows to servicemen and always smoked a cigar on stage. In the Universal film *Follow the Boys* he sawed Marlene Dietrich in half!

A turn-of-the-century *art nouveau* cigar urn, designed in Paris and filled with Havanas.

Top: Caricature dating back to 1842 and depicting the "tobacco craze" of the period.   Bottom: Caricature of famed pianist Artur Rubinstein, who never smoked on stage but once owned a tobacco plantation in Cuba and grew his own.

A woman selling cigars at the World's Columbian Exposition in Chicago in 1893.

SPÉCIMEN DE LA MARQUE DE LA RÉGIE FRANÇAISE.

TABACS

MANUFACTURES

DE L'ÉTAT

REPUBLIQUE FRANÇAISE

Marque déposée.

Z. DAVIDOFF

le spécialiste mondial du cigare

Top: Official tobacco seal of the Republic of France. Bottom: Z. Davidoff, cigar in hand and mouth, peering out from behind his own personalized cigar band.

Z. Davidoff behind the main counter of his tobacco shop in Geneva, Switzerland.
Davidoff's store serves as a cosmopolitan rendezvous for the cigar set.

AMSTERDAM.
Virginie Tabak by
Ibring & Puppe

Early seventeenth-century tobacco seal advertising Virginia plantation crops.

The Cubans originated the art of decorating cigar bands and cigar boxes. Here are two American versions designed by the Halpern Cigar Company.

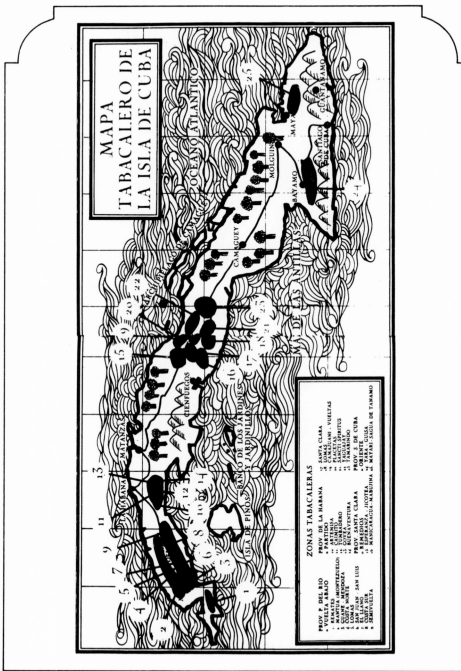

A map of Cuba showing the most important tobacco plantations. The richest and best leaves come from the area called *Vuelta Abajo*.

Decorations for cigar boxes of two American brands. The bottom design features the crest of the cigar company mounted on a bed of tobacco leaves.

Top: Ornate cigar box decoration depicting the "Glory of Cuba." Bottom: Cuban Government tobacco seal, required on all Havanas for export.

A variety of Havana cigars with decorated bands. The cigar band was reportedly invented by Gustave Bock, a Dutchman who was one of the first Europeans to cultivate a tobacco plantation in Cuba.

Top: A half wheel of cigars tied with a ribbon bearing the brand name of the cigar company. Bottom: Traditional decorative cigar box trim.

Originality as well as ornateness contribute to the "art" of the cigar band. Here is a special "American Presidents" series of bands.

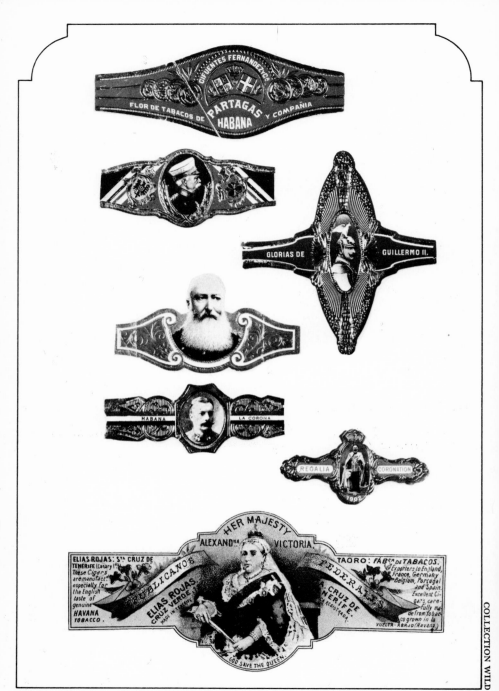

This collection of cigar bands features fine detail in design and lettering. A favorite ornamentation is a portrait in the center of the band.

A sample of cigar band portraits, including one of King Solomon and of Edward VII.

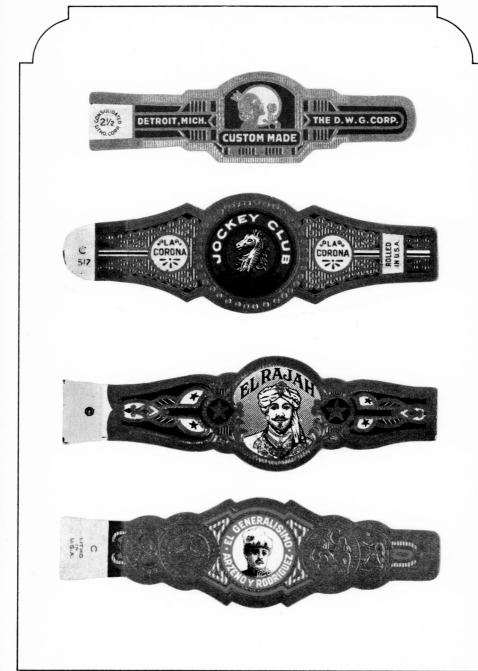

A group of richly decorated bands for American cigars.

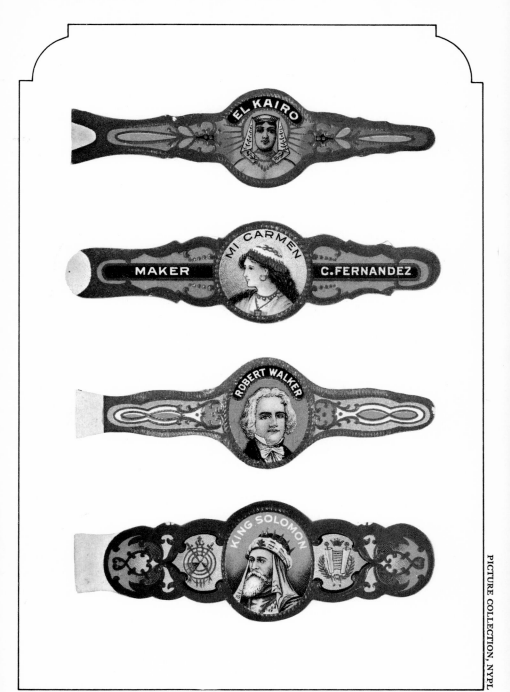

These bands feature more portraits and intricate patterns and crests.

Two ornate designs for the inside of cigar boxes.

The design for Lafayette cigars which appears on the inside and outside of the cigar box.

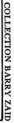

Cigar box design for Pink Pearl cigars.

Inside of cigar box, Madame Butterfly cigars.

A collection of old matchbox covers, showing a variety of designs and lettering. The decorating of matchbox covers became as much of a popular art form as that of the cigar box and the cigar band.

These matchbox covers show both elaborately drawn portraits as well as representational figures.

O ye *Jiggs,* O ye cigars!

which is performed by experts. The lightest cigars are placed to the right. It is necessary to arrange them so that the thin veins, which appear from time to time on the wrappers, will be placed underneath. . . . There are boxes of one hundred cigars, fifty, twenty-five, ten. Certain cigars benefit from individual boxes. Next, the boxes themselves are decorated. They may be decorated in a luxurious fashion (for certain smokers, there are special inlay masterpieces). But, in any case, the interior of the boxes is made of Cuban cedar from the countryside, a material which has a protective and preservative quality that has never been matched.

Each box will carry the guarantee of the Cuban state. I will say again that the quality undoubtedly fell at the beginning of the Castro age (with the attempt to produce a "popular cigar"), but it has now reached new heights. After a period of wandering in the wilderness, the Cubans are again the masters of the tobacco plant. The period of anxiety is well over. Specialists in the Castro regime admit that the customs cannot be changed if the quality is to be maintained.

The box is now ready for the perilous trip called exportation. The cigar has gone through three principal stages of fermentation. Until the fourth, which is produced in the summer of the following year (within four or five months following its departure from the island), the cigar ought to be considered—and sold—as a fresh one. But by simply calculating the time needed for the trip (a cigar travels by boat; it is stored at departure and at arrival), it is evident that a "fresh cigar is a rare thing to find in a tobacco shop.

The cigar ought to be sold within several weeks of receipt or withheld from the market for twelve months. I have clients who demand that they be notified when each good shipment arrives so they can quickly obtain cigars that have no more than several months of age and have not entered the cycle which opens the fourth stage of fermentation. To smoke a fresh cigar is, then, a question of personal taste—and of planning. It is a different pleasure and a very special one for those who have visited Cuba. They are "closer" to the leaf. The cigar is more supple, tender and softer. This cigar is called in Cuba a "farm" cigar.

But wait. Within several weeks of its arrival, a fresh cigar will begin to "work." If a delay takes place, you must wait until after the stage of fermentation.

Remember this cardinal rule: A cigar that is not smoked when fresh ought to be smoked after it has "rested"—a year or so after it has been boxed.

How do you keep a cigar in good condition?

Neither you nor the cigar loses anything by waiting. Whether stored at a cigar store or at home, a cigar ought always to be kept in the best conditions of humidity: between sixty degrees of humidity (minimum limit) and sixty-seven degrees (maximum limit). Do not go beyond these limits.

By chance you might have a natural storage place for cigars—a basement or storm cellar which would match that possessed by my Cuban friend with the twenty-five-year-old cigar. But probably not.

A Havana conserves itself in its box. Some people have advised opening it and, after taking one cigar, allowing the others to "breathe more easily." This is wrong. On the contrary, I completely trust the expert who wrote: "The best Havanas ought to live together. Their maturation stays even and they compensate each other." Cuban cedar is conducive to aging; you should keep your cigars, then, piled up in their boxes.

In my Geneva store I have installed humidors in which the temperature and hygrometrical degrees are constantly controlled. In the numerous cellars where my reserves are kept, I have installed instruments that permit me to regulate the surrounding temperature and humidity. I have had occasion, over the years, to watch the "work" of the cigar, to measure its successive annual periods of fermentation, their reduction in time, and to determine the optimum conditions for conservation. It is necessary to realize, and this I can't repeat often enough, that a cigar kept under good conditions not only does not lose any of its quality but actually becomes better. In aging, it becomes different, but no less satisfying. It acquires its full maturity.

Many men prefer newly vintaged Beaulojais to a wine kept for some time in a cellar. It is their taste—and their right. Others, on the other hand, care only for aged wines, those that have been stored for some time. So it is with the cigar. If a fresh cigar is often difficult to find, a year-old Havana is not. Some people prefer to wait two, three, five years or more. Under good conditions of humidity and temperature, you lose nothing in waiting. For some smokers, the cigar gains, with time, a supplementary bouquet, a deeper resonance—what lovers of vintage wines call body. Certain cigars do not do so well, for all cigars do age somewhat differently. These are the cigars you cannot store for more than two or three or four years without their losing their aroma. Which are they? You will have to consult your cigar merchant. Make him your confidant.

It is very difficult to sell a cigar. It calls for profound judgment, true experience, deep wisdom. How many times have I heard merchants who do not deserve this title formulate contradictory answers, give their clients most ridiculous advice. It does not matter to some of them so long as they sell a cigar. It is pure cheap showmanship for anyone who knows something about the cigar.

The buyer is totally in the hands of the seller if he is a rank amateur. Only the seller—regardless of the buyer's expertise— is in a position to know if the merchandise he suggests has been in storage for twelve, twenty-four, forty-eight months or more, if it is in a period of fermentation or has reached maturity, if the cigar is still aging or ought to be, if it is at the maximum of its potential for quality, if it will improve or change.

The merchant is omniscient. His word is not to be doubted.

It is his role to give the buyer some advice on keeping cigars in good condition:

"You will be able to keep the cigar a year, or more, if you have a good storeroom or humidor. This one here can be smoked within three months. This other box ought not to be opened before next winter...."

How many stupid things have I heard in the course of my trips! One day, in New York, I observed a merchant advising a heavy-set client to store his cigars in a freezer! He swore that he could keep them in good condition indefinitely. I wonder if the merchant did?

If you want to keep cigars under the best conditions and build a generous, appropriate reserve, choose a good merchant very, very carefully. I do not plead sainthood. I am not the only good cigar merchant in the world. But I believe that there are too few who merit this title.

To know how to buy, and from whom to buy, is then the first requirement. To learn how to treat the cigars in storage comes next. One error, and everything can be irremediably spoiled!

STORAGE ROOM OR CELLAR FOR CIGARS

Every lover of cigars should possess a "humidor" in his home, a shelter where the cigars are well preserved and stored for several months before being smoked.

The principal place to store them is in a cellar. Is is there that the cigars "sleep." To be sure, the ideal is to have at your disposition a cellar where the humidity is maintained constantly within the right limits (betwen sixty and sixty-seven degrees of humidity) and where the temperature stays constantly from sixty-eight to seventy-seven degrees. That you may find in an old house or you can install a humidifier. But natural conditions are rare, very rare. Usually, in Europe and in other northern climates, the seasonal variations are so great that preservation becomes difficult and costly.

KEEPING YOUR CIGARS

What then do you do? The ideal solution consists, evidently, in installing a room or a nook where the special conditions can be realized. This is what the English call a maturing room. I don't think that anyone in the world except true professionals has facilities of this sort.

But there are, happily, other solutions. It is important to know before seeking a solution that the Havana does not need to be constantly maintained under tepid and humid conditions. It is able to "sleep" (so long as the variations in temperature and humidity are not *too* great) like a wine. It will "work" subtly. In August, in the first years, it will exude its "flower." Restored several times to a humid and tepid atmosphere, it will recover its suppleness, all its qualities. This is the cardinal rule of preserving cigars. With a supply in a special cellar and a box in the house (cigars to be smoked during the week), the true devotee of the cigar can be considered fit for any test or occasion.

RULE: A stay of only several weeks in a "humidor" will suffice in order for a dry cigar to recover its suppleness and to give the best of its potential. If a Havana has not been brutalized, it should be able, over the years, to pull out of its lethargy. This is because the cigar never ceases to mature.

THE HUMIDOR

Each true smoker should have a box (the dimensions will vary according to his needs) in his home in which he keeps, close at hand, perfect cigars ready to smoke.

The smallest "humidor" is the cigar box itself. If you want, replace one of the cigars with a glass tube open at each end and furnished with a sponge that you dampen regularly. The evaporation suffices to maintain the right humidity. You can find such tubes—adapted to the size of the box—at all cigar stores of distinction.

There are humidors that will hold fifty, one hundred, two hundred fifty, or five hundred cigars. They are, in general, boxes of walnut or oak, tightly closed, lined with leather or plastic material. Some of them, made in Spain, are made in the shape of pirate's chests. Their price is not beyond reach. In the inside you will find one or more metallic tubes for humidifying, and they are easy to use. You ought to fill them with water (or moisten them, if that's required) once a month. They contain a sponge or a porous stone.

Naturally, the chest ought to be placed in a spot where the temperature is constant—not too high or too low. If you wish, you might transform a chest or a cupboard into a humidor by placing strips of leather around the openings to increase air-tightness. Also adapt one or two tubes of the current type for humidifying. With attention to temperature and humidity, you will possess a place for cigars where they will recover their suppleness, their youth, their aroma.

If you bring cigars from the cellar or "maturing room," let them stay in a humidor at least one or two months before smoking. If they rest longer, all the better. Avoid, to whatever measure you can, moving cigars from the humidor to the cellar and back to the humidor. A Havana is a happy infant, but it does call for straightforward treatment.

TO BUILD A RESERVE OF CIGARS

The problem of stock—the personal reserve—has caused the spilling of much ink and has started many discussions. At the beginning of this century, before the introduction of that most logical solution for storage, the humidor, it was hardly possible to keep any large quantity of cigars in the home.

Twenty-four boxes—five hundred cigars—constituted a royal supply. This was the number recommended by Eugene Marsan, who added, "Do not let them spoil. It is necessary to keep the boxes in a closed iron chest, and do not add more than three or four boxes at a time. . . ." Later, around 1920, when the cigar fancier had dreamed of maintaining the humidity in a confined atmosphere, Sacha Guitry advanced the number of one thousand cigars for a reserve—this figure including those cigars currently being smoked.

Today, thanks to the glass tubes for humidifying, there is no longer a problem of quantity. There is no ideal stock, but, rather, a supply adapted to your tastes, your needs. Conscious of this fact, I have, however, to simplify the problem, divided the mass of cigar smokers into three categories: the average smoker, the enlightened smoker who receives many friends, and, finally, the great lover of cigars, president of something, a rich maharajah, a big social celebrity. I will also take note of Mr. Everyman, the occasional smoker who conserves his cigars—when he has them.

The reader can fit himself into one of these categories or invent an intermediate one.

The Average Smoker. This is the client who makes up the majority of smokers. His stock is composed of four hundred to one thousand cigars (fifteen to forty boxes), and he replaces them one hundred by one hundred. The oldest in his reserve are three years old. If he is able to keep any for five years, all the better. On the advice of his merchant, he could add cigars that age more slowly and thereby satisfy all tastes. In his humidor he will always have around fifty cigars to be smoked.

The Enlightened Smoker. He is a man who regularly receives friends, who enjoys holding before them a generous, rich, and luxurious selection. "It is not until after a Havana," Maurice des Ombiaux has written, "that the master of the house who has treated his friends is able to say as did Horace, 'I have completed a monument more durable than stone.' " This model host possesses from eight hundred to two thousand cigars—at least twenty-four boxes—and a complete selection of lengths, shapes, types, tastes, brands. He knows how to speak about his cigars. He is acquainted with their subtle resources, their true purpose; he

THE CONNOISSEUR'S BOOK OF THE CIGAR

knows how to announce the pleasures that can be anticipated. He is an artist of the cigar. At his disposition in a humidor should be one hundred to two hundred cigars.

The Great Lover. As with all passion, that which inspires the escape represented by the cigar can only be tentatively measured. There is no limit to the resources a man can consume—especially if you multiply the potential by the number of a man's friends and those others who surround him.

Some of my clients buy a thousand cigars a month. Without doubt they distribute the larger part of them, deriving pleasure (or profit) from this largesse. But these reserves are good for them, even if the cigars they keep are destined for others. They survey their reserve with special care; spiritually, they walk among them as does a proprietor of vineyards in his fields, the lover of art among his paintings, a collector among his statues. They leave to no one the primordial task of watching their "humidor," which is not a box but a piece of furniture in which can be found five hundred or a thousand cigars, or more. They are aware of the maturation process required by the very best Havanas, and these they have consigned to "work" in silence. During the month of August, when the tobacco fever rises, they are even more attentive. In writing these lines, I think of Prince Saddrudin Aga Khan, whose stock at the Château of Bellerive is truly one for a prince, of the Barons Elie and Edmond de Rothschild, of the banker Gerard Pereire, of M. de Roquemaurel, of M. Leclery, of Darryl Zanuck—who, under Battista, possessed his own Cuban plantation.

The Occasional Smoker. I say that he is a beginner. He does not smoke regularly but only when the fancy strikes him, or perhaps on some occasion—an anniversary, a trip, or the like—when a cigar is presented to him as a gift.

Eventually, he should stock thirty to forty cigars—and as many of the precious, rare ones as he can. He can use the humidifying tubes or a small humidor.

KEEPING YOUR CIGARS

WHAT CIGARS TO KEEP IN RESERVE?

The composition of a reserve, whether simple or princely, is above all a question of taste, of personal choice. You can discuss without end the respective merits of different cigars, by their length, their age, their type, their origin. It is necessary to discuss them. It is also part of the pleasure.

The reserve I propose has no more value than that of an example. It is, within reasonable limits, the reflection of my personal taste or that of a cigar lover who has my tastes. It consists of more than two thousand cigars, of which more than half are Havanas. A supply that contained all the Havanas would have more than forty thousand cigars. It is unimaginable, just as one cannot envisage a wine cellar that would contain all the great crûs of the world.

If is, then, necessary to choose. Here is my choice:

1. I base my selection, you will understand, on my own personally chosen Châteaux—the excellent Davidoff—because they represent already a choice rigorously made and renewed each year by taking account of the latest leaf from different plantations in the sacrosanct Vuelta. These Châteaux, which cover the array of Coronas, are the fine flower of the great brands. I produced the first Château—the Château-Margaux—in 1945 with the aid of the Hoyo de Monterrey firm and I continue that association.

All the Châteaux are excellent cigars which age well, within their scope, and which offer the smoker a full store of surprises.

Two small Coronas .... Château Haut-Brion
　　　　　　　　　　　　　　　　　　　　　　　Château-Laffitte
Two average Coronas .... Château-Margaux
　　　　　　　　　　　　　　　　　　　　　　　Château-Latour
A large Corona (5½" long; ¾" in diameter)..... Château-Yquem

My Châteaux are not sold in a box, but in a case. They are bunched, without band or cellophane, and tied together with a silk ribbon. This packaging, I feel, assists their aging. They

69

breathe more easily than in a box, and help each other out.

2. On a foundation of the Châteaux—*noblesse oblige*—I would place several boxes of cigars made by Rey del Mundo. The cigars made by this distinguished firm do not have the reputation of others more celebrated but they are a pledge of taste and refinement.

In the categories of Demi-tasse, small Corona, and Corona, Rey del Mundo offers some marvelous cigars that are lighter—in their entirety—than my Châteaux, and of a paler color that remains even after maturation.

These are excellent cigars for all occasions, light but full-bodied and of an aroma which is complete and always satisfying.

3. To complete the solemn selection of Châteaux and of the Rey del Mundo, I will choose some Lonsdales Belinda. These are excellent cigars with a darker dress and more body than the Rey del Mundo; virile cigars, which go well with an important dinner or some major occasion.

4. A judicious collection ought to include some of the less classic types such as thin and long Panatelas, short Panatelas, and Demi-tasse, so as to enable you to satisfy the tastes of all, including women and young smokers.

I would mention, for these categories, Rey del Mundo, Rafael Gonzales, Partagas, Punch, Romeo y Julieta, Montecristo, Belinda, Ramón Allones, Upmann, Hoyo de Monterrey.

All the Havana brands are, I repeat, excellent ones. A personal selection of their products, one dicated by your taste, cannot but enrich your collection.

One important detail. Be sure that the Havanas you stock are indeed Havanas. If you are not careful, you will fall victim to certain deceptions. False Havanas are not rare. A number of countries manufacture cigars (Germany, the Netherlands, Switzerland, Belgium among them) that they claim to be Havanas. Sometimes, in effect, a small amount of Cuban tobacco has been imported and used in the filler. At other times, there is not a drop of Cuban tobacco to be found. In any case, these cigars have no right to the title of Havana. They have none of its qualities—none of the fineness, the perfume, or the singular virtue of continuing to "live."

You ought also to note the names of those Cuban brands which, since the rise of Castro, are manufactured outside the country. They are sometimes sold as Havanas and packaged in a way that is traditionally Cuban. They may be products manufactured with Florida tobacco or that of the Canary Islands.

Henry Clay (now planted in the Canary Islands) has changed its name; its owners have struck the new name of Don Miguel, and they get the best that can be drawn from the Canaries. La Corona, Bock, Cabanas, Villar y Villar, Murias, all members of the group *Tabacalera americana,* tody produce products of lesser quality than before. That does not mean, however, that they can be eliminated from a list of good cigars in any absolute fashion.

It is necessary to admit that American cigars satisfy the taste of today's public for the light, refreshing cigar which can be smoked at any time or place without much effort.

These cigars, which are especially light, rather colorless, easy to smoke, are aromatized, washed, and treated for those who demand no more from a cigar than they would from one or two cigarettes. The success of the American cigar—this candy!—started long before the blockade of Cuba. Americans have never been (relatively) great customers of Havanas. The total figure of their importations (the last was nine years ago) never passed more than a figure of twenty-five million a year. Here are the current figures of production and exportation:

Total production ....around 700 million
Exportation ....around 80 million
(*You will note the importance of the Cuban national consumption; almost 9/10ths of the production.*)

71

Countries that import cigars:

Spain ....around 40 million
England ....around 25 million
Switzerland/France ....around 10 million
Rest of the world ....around 5 million

The fashion for colorless cigars was born in America and expanded beyond those boundaries long ago. It gave birth, in Cuba, to the *double claro* (or *clarissimo*). The factories of the American-owned *Tabacalera* produced the first specimens. At one time, I thought for a moment that the *Tabacalera double claro* was going to revolutionize the market. But it soon appeared clear that it would not find a large market in places other than the United States. Neither the Cubans nor the Spanish nor the English would accept this cigar, which is cut too short, dries too quickly, and has little taste, aroma, or perfume. Even if the Cuban *double claro* has won the right to be listed in the catalogues of first-rate Cuban cigarmakers, it has not attained the popularity in sales of the other categories.

In America, by contrast, the sales figures of these treated cigars have never ceased to climb, and the manufacturers have gone a long way in developing techniques to subdue the tobacco. Some of their cigars are made with homogenized paper; that is to say they are wrapped in a sort of paper made with waste paper that has been pounded and blended. Some of these cigars are exported to Europe. Their lightness and sweetness has won them a certain audience. You judge for yourself. Their names?

Hava Tampa (which come from Florida)
Robert Burns (famed for the cigarillos)
Dutch Master
King Edward
House of Windsor
Casanovas

OTHER CIGARS

At the time of the visit of former West German Chancellor

72

Ludwig Erhard to Paris, I received, one morning, a telephone call from the Elysée Palace.

"Monsieur Davidoff," said an anxious voice. "We have some Havanas but it appears that the Chancellor smokes no other cigars than those of Brazil. . . . Do you know what brand he prefers?"

I did not have to think for more than a moment. "Suerdick, almost certainly. I will get you some boxes on the next plane."

I was not mistaken. I do not think that the Brazilian cigars are among the great ones; they do not rival the Havanas in taste, perfume, or aroma. But there is among them a hierarchy, and certain great smokers prefer them to Havanas. In addition to the Suerdick, there are also the cigars of the Cruz de Almas (Bahia region) and the small Talvis.

Philippines
In Manila some cigars are produced which have ardent defenders, certainly those that carry the names Flor de Isabela and Alhambra.

Mexico
Ornellas, La Prueba, Costenos

Jamaica
Macanudos, Tropical de Luxe

Puerto Rico
La Restina

Canary Islands
Don Miguel, Don Diego, Flamenco

Cigars of Europe:
Holland: Schimmelpenninck, Panter
Denmark: E. Nobel, Hirschprung

All tastes, most definitely, are part of nature and are respectable. "All cigars finish in smoke," said an old Brazilian wiseman. But they are not the same cigars; and it is not the same smoke.

Havanas ought to make up the base or foundation of your collection. Other cigars do not live. As members of the silent and secret orchestra that you will direct, they cannot match the precious products of the famous island in tone and brilliance.

PART FOUR

The Gotha of the Cigar

Some personalities are so associated with the cigar that it is impossible not to cite them in a book of this sort. Famed smokers, great scholars, celebrated merchants, inspired commentators—they constitute the glory and the legend of the Havana.

I have not hesitated to mix in names from the past with those from recent times or the present. This rapprochement does not embarrass me. The cigar obliterates time. My name appears among those listed because, above all, it is a rallying point for all lovers of the cigar.

ALLENDY (DOCTOR)

Author of the most interesting *Psychoanalysis of the Smoker,* a book that emphasizes the symbolic significance of the cigar as a sign both of virility and of comfort.

AZTECS

In his work *La vie quotidienne au temps des Azteques à la veille de la conquête espagnole,* Jacques Soustelle points out that the cigar was used in Montezuma's court. The fat aromatic torches they smoked then (and from which they could gain almost immediate sleep) were, however, very far, in both appearance and taste, from those we smoke today. The tobacco contained a mixture of hallucinogenic elements (mushrooms, etc.).

The cigar played a special role in the religion and medicine of the natives; priests smoked it during certain special ceremonies. At the time of the arrival of Cortes in 1519, cigar smoking was the special privilege of priests and of noblemen.

BALZAC, HONORÉ DE

He did not like the cigar, contrary to the thought of certain characters in his novels: Colonel Chabert (*Le Colonel Chabert,* 1852), upon his return from exile consecrated the first seconds of his new life to the purchase of cigars.

BANVILLE, THEODORE DE (FRENCH POET, 1823–1891)

In *The Soul of Paris* he prophesied the disappearance of ciga-
ettes, then a new, absurd fashion, and the ascendancy of the cigar
as something much more practical.

BOCK, GUSTAVE

A Dutchman, one of the first Europeans to cultivate a tobacco
plantation in Cuba. The invention of the cigar band is loosely
attributed to him. He wrote the first succinct *Art of Smoking
the Cigar*.

BYRON, LORD

The first poet to have written an ode to the cigar, this one inspired by an adventure from *Mutiny on the Bounty*—"Sublime
Tobacco," which ends with the line, "Give me a cigar!"

CASANOVA

One of the first Europeans to evoke the cigar in a literary work,
in his *Mémoires*. He presented the *cigarito* to his contemporaries
and said that since it did not offend the ladies it certainly did
not offend him. He also declared himself, however, one of the
first wicked proponents of the cigarette.

CHAMBRUN, COMTE DE

A descendant of La Fayette, he is considered by many today one
of the greatest European connoisseurs of the cigar.

CHAPLIN, CHARLIE

In the last episode of *The Gold Rush* he made two generations
cry with his delighted discovery of the chewed stub of a cigar
abandoned by a millionaire—the symbolic act of the little man
who is never able to forget that he is poor.

CHATEAUBRIAND, FRANÇOIS-RENÉ DE

He wondered if one should write *une segarre* (feminine) or *un segar* (masculine) and seemed very impatient to discover this new fad from Spain (1812).

CHURCHILL, SIR WINSTON

During the Blitz a German bomb destroyed the Dunhill shop in London. At two o'clock in the morning, having inspected the damage, the manager of the shop rushed to the phone to inform Churchill, "Your cigars are safe, sir."

Churchill discovered the cigar during the time of the Spanish-American war. He was no more than twenty years old. According to certain authorities, he smoked more than three hundred thousand cigars in his lifetime.

Provided with cigars by his colleagues and admirers, he regularly sent those left over to his friend Sibelius, the great Finnish composer, who also died an octogenarian. Churchill usually smoked no more than half a cigar, sometimes double Coronas and all sorts of the finest Havana choices of a dark tobacco, with a band bearing his picture. Certain of the Havanas were named Churchill by the makers. He was also seen to choose Lonsdales as well as Panatelas.

The cigar played a role in his political career. During the electoral campaign of June 1945, Labour party politicians reproached him for so regularly smoking expensive cigars when the people had to queue up to buy a package of cigarettes. In 1947 a Labour member of the House of Lords, Lord Chorley, recommended that Churchill be deprived of cigars for two years as punishment for his severe denunciations of the majority (Labour) leaders. Put to a voice vote, the motion was defeated.

At another time, a resident of Margate revealed plans for a monument to the glory of Churchill, a gigantic statue, cigar in hand, to be raised on the cliffs of Dover. The glowing cigar ash was to serve as a revolving lighthouse beacon for ships at sea. This proposal was also quashed. There are, however, more modest statues that represent Churchill with a double Corona between his teeth. This same image is to be found in a stained-glass window of the parish church of Cransley.

To Viscount Montgomery, who told him one day: "I do not drink. I do not smoke. I sleep a great deal. That is why I am in one-hundred-per-cent form," Churchill responded, "I drink a great deal. I sleep little, and I smoke cigar after cigar. That is why I am in two-hundred-per-cent form."

CLAY, HENRY

A label that disappeared from Cuba at the time of the diplomatic rupture with Castro along with other marks of the *Tabacalera americana*. Who was Henry Clay? He may have been the famous American senator, who possessed financial interests in Cuba. I have looked this up but can find no verification.

CONSOLIDATED CIGAR CORPORATION

The largest company in America that specializes in the sale of cigars. In their New York port warehouses—entirely automated and air-conditioned—are stored nearly five million cigars.

DAVIDOFF

The name of a person of Slavic origin who was chosen to write these lines and who runs a unique shop, which he owns, in Geneva, Switzerland—40, rue du Marché. It is a cosmopolitan rendezvous for great cigar smokers and one of the best smoking shops in the world. For several years this shop has been the sole depository for the famous Châteaux cigars. These cigars never fail to capture the fine flower of each year's tobacco crop from the Vuelta Abajo.

Zino Davidoff, called by journalists "Your Man in Havana," promulgated the idea that commerce in cigars, like that of wine, called for continual study and adaptation to changing circumstances. In Cuba, as in the wine region of Bordeaux, there are good and bad years. For example:

THE GOTHA OF THE CIGAR

Good harvest years 1958–59

1964–65

Poor harvest year 1945

(caused by the appearance of the parasite Motto Azul)

The best leaves are not always found in the same fields, but are always found in the Vuelta Abajo. Davidoff's secret (and that of his Châteaux) is a deep knowledge of all the acres of the sacred square of Vuelta Abajo. For the wrapper, he considers best El Corojo, San Luis de Vuelta Abajo, the leaf from the territory of Hoyo de Monterrey.

But, in the matter of cigar tobacco as in life, one ought always to be ready to revise ideas and judgment.

DELPIERRE, ANTOINE

A French privateersman who, in 1793, broke the British blockade of Boulogne. He captured a Dutch ship carrying cigars. These were distributed to the residents of Boulogne. But, according to Monsieur Lemoigne, French Chief Inspector of Tobacco and one of the Frenchmen most cultivated in the history of the cigar, the cigar made its entry into France in a different manner: Revolutionary soldiers brought it back from war in Spain, where the factories of Seville were then flourishing.

DON JUAN

Mérimée (the author of *Carmen*) told the story of Don Juan one day meeting the devil, who was traveling along the opposite bank of the river Guadalquivir. Insolent by nature, Don Juan took out a cigar and called for a light. The devil smiled and reached his arm out from one bank to the other. His fingers held a burning torch by which Don Juan, hiding his fright in stupor, lighted his Seville cigar.

DUFY, RAOUL

Many of his paintings he has exchanged for cigars. At the end of his life he does not wish more money!

DUNHILL

The greatest name in the English-speaking cigar world. The founder of the dynasty, Alfred H. Dunhill, gave the Havana the renown it deserves, and his descendants have carried on his ideas. He wrote an interesting book entitled *The Gentle Art of Smoking*. Today the Dunhill firm, unanimously respected, carries all the needs of the smoker, including perfume, and has fans throughout the world. In the London and New York shops are found the humidor rooms for Havanas. The shops are irreproachable.

EDWARD VII OF ENGLAND

His mother, Queen Victoria, had banned the smoking of cigars in her presence, and, by extension, anywhere in high society. Her son, the Prince of Wales, broke this ban. On the day he assumed the throne as Edward VII, he uttered these words in Court. "Gentlemen, you may smoke." His royal preference was the double Corona, and his personal band (long sought by collectors) is decorated with three white plumes. Whoever has this rare item in his collection can pride himself for being on familiar terms with a king.

FAROUK

A famous cigar smoker and a lover of large models. One day he entered the Davidoff shop in Geneva, preceded by his bodyguards, and asked a curious question: "I have fifteen thousand cigar bands of double Coronas in reserve. Can you furnish me with the right cigars?"

They were furnished to him. He returned several times and, passing the time, would ask questions about that year's crop. He never bought fewer than five thousand cigars at a time.

FOCH, MARSHAL

He said that a good cigar cleared his mind and sharpened his judgment when he had to make an important decision on the eve of an offensive.

FREUD, SIGMUND

The famed founder of psychoanalysis was always with a cigar. He smoked continually while interpreting the dreams of his patients and, despite the advice of his doctors, was never able to do without them.

GARCÍA GALLO

He wrote the treaty that authorized the exportation of Havana cigars. Issued under Battista, it was recently reissued under the authority of Fidel Castro.

GLENN, COLONEL JOHN

The American astronaut who, upon his return from outer space, received the equivalent of his weight in Havana cigars even though their importation had been officially forbidden in his country.

GREENE, GRAHAM

The celebrated author of *Our Man in Havana*. The book makes no mention of the cigar—a tour de force if there ever was one.

GULBENKIAN

The cigar is part of the panoply of the oil magnates. The present holder of the Gulbenkian fortune has a personal agreement with the Partagas firm, an agreement Castro rendered void. Gulbenkian stocked up again via Prague and arranged payments through a Soviet bank. To those who are astonished to see this capitalistic kingmaker smoking the cigars of the Castro regime, he replies: "Even if the devil were to take possession of the Vuelta, I would continue to smoke Havanas!"

HEMINGWAY, ERNEST

Devoted smoker of Havana cigars; the smoke of a Corona took for him the place of Proust's sugar cake. One day he presented Ava Gardner a cigar band as a souvenir of their first meeting.

HUGO, VICTOR

In the cigar factories of Cuba, his works have long been favorites. You can still hear the stories being read aloud. Poet Robert Desnos, visiting Cuba in 1928, was surprised to discover that some workers knew part of Hugo's poetry by heart.

KIPLING, RUDYARD

Placed high value on the cigar—perhaps too high. "If Maggie does not wish to have a rival, then I do not wish to marry Maggie," he wrote, referring to his daily cigar. He is also the author of this celebrated sentence, often quoted: "A woman is only a woman, but a good cigar is a Smoke."

KREUGER, IVAR

The king of matches and a great financier. Kreuger killed himself after having smoked his last double Corona. The owner of seven apartments in Paris, he sat in the most private one smoking Havanas selected from a special humidor.

LA ROCHEFOUCAULD-LIANCOURT, DUC DE

He is the author of the oldest known eulogy in French to the cigar (at that time called the *segar*). Around 1794, the Duke was sent on a special mission to America to present a message from the French revolutionary government. The following moving text is to be found in the report of his voyage:

> The cigar is a great resource. It is necessary to have traveled for a long time on a ship to understand that at least the cigar affords you the pleasure of smoking. It raises your spirits. Are you troubled by something? The cigar will dissolve it. Are you subject to aches and pains (or bad temper)? The cigar will change your disposition. Are you harassed by unpleasant thoughts? Smoking a cigar puts one in a frame of mind to dispense with these. Do you ever feel a little faint from hunger? A

THE GOTHA OF THE CIGAR

cigar satisfies the yearning. If you are obsessed by sad thoughts, a cigar will take your mind off them. Finally, don't you sometimes have some pleasant remembrance or consoling thought? A cigar will reinforce this. Sometimes they die out, and happy are those who do not need to relight too quickly. I hardly need to say anything more about the cigar, to which I dedicate this little eulogy for past services rendered.

LAS CASAS, BARTOLOMÉ

The first chronicler of the discovery of the cigar and of the Spanish Conquest of the New World. In his *Istoria de las Indias,* he pays tribute to the cigar: "If you smoke too much, you will become drunk as with a strong wine. . . . I found this out for myself."

LISZT, FRANZ

He was never without his personal supply, carried in an immense wooden box with three layers. He said, "A good Cuban cigar closes the door to the vulgarities of the world." At the end of his life, about the time when he was to enter a monastery, he asked, and obtained, the right to smoke cigars as he pleased—a practice he continued until his dying day.

LOWELL, AMY

A formidable woman of great talent. A poet and critic, author of "Patterns" and "Lilacs," she was the Imagist member of a famous Boston family. A cigar was sometimes seen in her hands—or mouth.

MARSHALL, THOMAS

Native of Indiana, Vice-President of the United States under Woodrow Wilson from 1913 to 1921, he is known for only one utterance: "What this country needs is a really good five-cent cigar." Alas, inflation has destroyed any chance.

MARX, GROUCHO

The last surviving Marx brother. His experience was similar to

Kipling's. One day his wife asked him to give up cigars. He responded, "No, but we can remain good friends."

MAUGHAM, SOMERSET

A devoted student of the cigar, as this extract from his work, *Summing Up,* proves:

> A good Havana is one of the best pleasures that I know. At the time when I was young and very poor, I only smoked cigars which were offered to me. I promised myself that if I ever had some money that I would savor a cigar each day after lunch and after dinner. This is the only resolution of my youth that I have kept, and the only realized ambition which has not brought disillusion. I like a mild cigar, of delicate aroma and medium length. If the cigar is too small, you can not enjoy the smoke. If too fat, the smoke overwhelms you. The best cigar is one that you can roll without effort, that is wrapped in a leaf that does not dissolve in the mouth, and which keeps its aroma to the end. After the last puff, when you put the stubby butt out and the last smoke curls away, who does not marvel at the work, the complicated enterprise which has produced this half-hour of pleasure? Men have labored for years under the tropical sun and crossed the seven seas to bring this pleasure to your side.

MELVILLE, HERMAN

The famous author of *Moby-Dick* claimed that the Cuban climate gave to tobacco grown there the best aroma in the world and to the Cubans the most beautiful skin.

MENENDEZ

A great family of Havana who were the proprietors of Upmann and Montecristo (among other brands) and who today manufacture the Don Miguel in the Canary Islands.

MÉRIMÉE, PROSPER

The author of *Carmen,* he was captivated by the beautiful cigarette-cigar girls who worked in the Seville plants, especially the gypsy girls who had handled the imported leaves since the beginning of the eighteenth century. Their work, however, if one can believe the experts, was confined to the interior of the factories.

MUSSET, ALFRED DE

Famed French poet and a great cigar smoker, he wrote a great deal about the pleasures of the cigar—"The best way of killing time." He shared this passion (among others) with George Sand, the greatest of lady cigar smokers in history.

ONASSIS, ARISTOTLE

He shared with his friend and frequent guest Winston Churchill a liking for Havana cigars. He has fitted out his yacht *Christina* with a humidor. Unfortunately, the Havana is not a good sea voyager.

PALICIO

Famed maker of Havana cigars; owner of Hoyo de Monterrey and Punch. The heir to this great name is devoted to painting and the pleasures of Saint-Tropez.

PERDOMO, DR. JOSÉ

A Cuban. One of the most knowledgeable experts of the Havana. His research is authoritative. You can read his articles in the *Revue des Tabacs,* edited in Paris. It is an excellent publication for readers of French.

RAINIER OF MONACO

A true connoisseur of the cigar. He loves Château-Margaux and the Lonsdales of Rafael Gonzales. One day he told Onassis—then a business associate—that Onassis judged Havanas by their length. "And the Prince chooses them by their band," replied the ship-owner. Both men are truly great connoisseurs of the cigar.

RALEIGH, SIR WALTER

If one believes the chroniclers of the year 1618, he smoked a cigar on the executioner's block. His name is often linked with tobacco, especially that from Virginia.

RAVEL, MAURICE

A great lover of Havanas. Smoking cigars, he claimed, inspired his composing.

RENCURREL, BERNARDINO

The oldest of names inscribed at the registry of trademarks in Havana (1810). Thereafter, in the same registry, one finds:

```
1810   H. de Cabanas y Carbajol, said to have existed since 1797
1827   Partagas
1830   Mi Fama por el Orbe Vuelta, of José García
1834   Por Larranaga
1840   El Figaro de Julian Rovera
1844   H. Upmann
1845   La Corona
```

ROBINSON, EDWARD G.

American importers in 1949 presented him with the title "Mister Cigar" in recognition of the publicity he had given to the cigar. He chewed them a little too far—especially in the gangster movies—but off the screen he smoked them with much more decorum.

ROLFE, JOHN

A British citizen considered to be the first tobacco planter in the New World. Around 1610 he "harvested" leaves near Jamestown, Virginia. Married to the Indian princess Pocahontas, he returned to England, where she was received at Court. (He, a commoner, waited at the door.) Pocahontas died of consumption, and John Rolfe, like many fellow planters, soon remarried. His new wife

THE GOTHA OF THE CIGAR

was one of a group of bourgeois immigrants who used to pay storekeepers in casks of Virginia leaf tobacco.

ROTHSCHILD

Members of this distinguished family traditionally appreciate cigars of high quality. Baron Elie, of the French branch, orders two thousand Châteaux-Laffitte each year.

RUBINSTEIN, ARTUR

Famed pianist. He once possessed a tobacco plantation in Cuba and distributed to his friends cigars banded with his effigy.

SEVILLE

The royal factories of Seville were established in 1731, but cigars were manufactured in the city from 1676. Around 1800, five thousand workers handled the Cuban leaf in enormous workrooms. Théophile Gautier in *Voyage en Espagne,* Davillier in *Le Tour du monde,* and others described the boisterous, colorful, voluptuous world of the *fábrica.* In 1846, Prosper Mérimée published his *Carmen,* in which the heroine is the perfect symbol of the manufacturing plants.

Maurice Barrès evoked the images of the Seville cigar girls in his book *Du sang, de la volupté et de la mort* and, later, Pierre Louÿs in his *La Femme et le Pantin.*

Painters have also been attracted by the charm of the female cigar workers. One of them (if you can believe certain stories) served as a model for two of Goya's famous paintings, to be found in the Prado, *Maja vestida* and *Maja desnuda.* Gustave Doré did a number of etchings which depicted the plants.

Here are the cigar girls of Seville as seen by Pierre Louÿs:

> Those most dressed wear a blouse (they are the prudes); almost all work with their breasts exposed, wearing a simple cloth skirt which is sometimes tucked up around the thighs. There are some, to be sure, un-

attractive bodies among this group, but all were interesting and I stopped often before a most beautiful woman—with a full bosom, clear, shining skin. . . .

The cigar girls were also cigar smokers, Théophile Gautier points out:

> Some of them resolutely carried a cigar at an angle in their mouths with all the aplomb of a cavalry officer; others, O God, chewed tobacco like old sailors because they were allowed to have all the tobacco they wanted which could be consumed where they worked.

Beautiful or not, they disappeared from the scene at the beginning of this century.

STENDHAL

He expressed a special interest in the cigar, an interest that often cropped up in his work. For example, in his journal dated April 10, 1838, he speaks with respect of the young businessmen of Marseilles "who earn eight or ten thousand francs a day . . . [and who] carry cigars in their pockets."

Stendhal smoked Toscanis, manufactured in Italy or the Vatican City. Drily rolled, they give off an acrid smell. "On a cold morning in winter," Stendhal wrote, "a Toscan cigar fortifies the soul."

At this time, importing of Cuban-leaf cigars made in Seville was forbidden in Italy. In Spain, Mérimée had much better luck.

TWAIN, MARK

A celebrated cigar smoker. On the Mississippi he very quickly learned from the poker players the difference between a Havana cigar and those from Florida. He preferred the Havanas.

URBAN VIII

Reigned as Pope around 1640. He forbade, by papal bull, Spanish priests to smoke cigars.

THE GOTHA OF THE CIGAR

VICTORIA, QUEEN

She hated the cigar and forbade that they be smoked in her presence or by her entourage. She reinforced the stiff edicts of James I, one of the fiercest enemies of tobacco. The Sultan Ahmed, however, was worse. He cut off the nose of any of his subjects found smoking a cigar.

WARNER, JACK

He prefers the light tobacco, as do many Americans. He smoked a Panatela of Hoyo de Monterrey on the day he held, at the Palm Beach casino in Cannes, his famous *banco* of a hundred million francs. And he won. The slightly chewed cigar is conserved in a silver box as a souvenir of that day.

WAYNE, JOHN

One of the great cigar smokers of Hollywood. For Westerns, he had a special cigar made, one much larger than usual. These movie cigars are appreciated by fanatical fans of Westerns despite their acrid taste.

WELLES, ORSON

One of the most famous actors now in films. He always demands that you open a cigar box before he will buy. When refused, he grumbles but buys the whole box anyway. He has never complained about his purchases. His favorite cigar is the Montecristo of Por Larranaga.

WENUSCH

A contemporary German chemist (Hitler followed his work with much interest) who invented an extraordinary smoking machine that successfully duplicated the burning and aroma of a cigar. He tried to reconstitute the aroma of a Havana. He failed.

THE CONNOISSEUR'S BOOK OF THE CIGAR

WOOLF, VIRGINIA

British novelist and essayist, she added to the smoke of the Bloomsbury Group, as did her husband, Leonard.

XERES, RODRIGO DE

A companion of Columbus, he is considered the first Western discoverer of the cigar. On October 28, 1492, on what is now the territory of the Dominican Republic, he smoked a cigar. The first written record of this is found on November fifth of the same year in the logbook of Vincent Pinzón.

Jewish by origin, Xeres was later accused of sorcery and, according to legend, was thrown into a dungeon during an inquisition and there rotted.

For some time in Cuba, a Rodrigo-de-Xeres prize is given each year to the product which is found to be the glory of the Havana.

ZANUCK, DARRYL

A famous film producer and connoisseur of the cigar. He possessed, before the advent of Castro, interests in the plantations of the Vuelta Abajo. This American prefers full-bodied tobacco, the *colorado*.

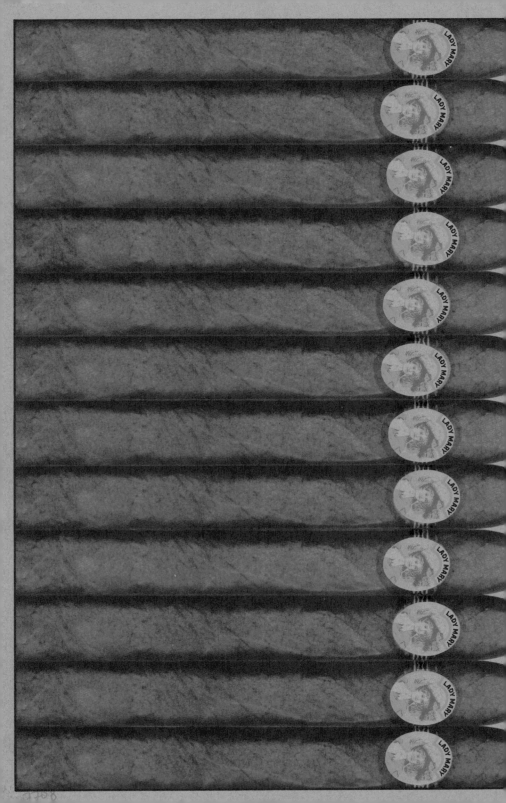